HOW TO BECOME A MILLIONAIRE

How to become a Millionaire

by

GERALD SPARROW

with illustrations by

IONICUS

ANTHONY BLOND

First published in September 1960
by Anthony Blond Ltd
34 Beech Street
London E.C.1

Second impression October 1960

Printed in Great Britain
by The Anchor Press, Ltd.,
Tiptree, Essex

CONTENTS

A WORD IN THE EAR OF YOUNG GENTLEMEN IN BRITAIN, THE COMMONWEALTH, AND ELSEWHERE WHO ARE DETERMINED TO BECOME MILLIONAIRES

There is one question which will surely be asked and which I hasten to answer.

If you know how to become a millionaire, why did you yourself not become one?

The answer is quite simple. I was not sufficiently determined. However, between 1941 and 1954 I did pursue money with a relentless zest, and, as a result, enjoyed a millionaire's income. Then, quite suddenly, all the money in the Far East seemed unimportant to me. What I wanted above all else was to live in Britain again.

So I have visited the promised land, but have not become a resident there. I know about wealth, have enjoyed it, but have not, by a lucky accident, become its captive. Such a person, I venture to suggest, is qualified to write this book.

The truth is, of course, that money goes to those who most passionately desire to possess it. There are, however, many tricks of the trade that will speed you on the way to millionairedom. You cannot learn everything from a book, but you can learn a great deal. If you do read this book carefully and acquire great wealth partly as a result of doing so, I shall be delighted to hear of your success.

GERALD SPARROW

Blackheath 1960

I

SET YOUR SIGHTS, ENTWISTLE

THIS little book, which, we hope, you will carry around with you, as you claw your way to the top, Entwistle, my boy, is exactly what its title says it is. It is a neat, brief guide on how to become a millionaire. If you follow the simple rules it suggests nothing can stop you. All the barriers, financial, social, psychological, between you and millionairedom can be overcome, or circumvented. You will arrive as surely as patrons converge on a pub at opening time.

You are still a young man, though the fact that you were born at 87 Paradise Road, Salford, in the County of Lancashire, may have made you older than your years. Locally 'educated', your father is something in the Post Office. Your mother is Scottish, bless her. And you, you only have one hard, clear ambition, to collect a million pounds. You are ruthlessly determined. That is all I ask. Dedicated, if you like. This slim volume will do the rest.

Now British business, including Big Business, is packed with nepotism, backscratching, old-school ties and the general flotsam of feudalism, but it has one great redeeming feature. It never keeps a man out if he is really good enough.

It is a fortress, a formidable one. You wish to break in. Now you are on the outside, that most unimportant of creatures, a young man looking for a job.

Yet you have advantages. You are honest. That is to say you will never commit a crime. You are good-looking in an undistinguished way. You are not a drunkard. Nor, thank God, are you a homosexual. If

You are good looking in an undistinguished way...

you had been we should have had to divert you to the Theatre or TV, where your oddity would have been a positive advantage.

You have common sense inherited from your mother, the gift of seeing a situation clearly without sentiment or prejudice, and of summing up the pros and cons in a forthright, useful way. You are methodical. This useful trait comes, apparently, from the old man. And from him, too, you derive an acceptable degree of humour, the degree that is welcome in British business circles – just enough to enable you to appreciate other people's jokes, but not enough to place you in any danger of becoming a wit – and embarrassing everybody.[1]

You are determined. This is your chief asset. You have set your sights with precision, and the image that you see is bright and clear. To have a million pounds in the bank, or, at least that, in shares and property, you will be 'worth a million'. So that in the fascinating column, 'Other people's money', when your estate has been valued for probate, there will be this laudable obituary – in addition to the Quickie Obit of the *Telegraph* and *The Times*:

Sir John Hardcastle Entwistle, of Leith Hall,

---

[1] Anglo-American business is so interlocked these days that it may be worth observing that British and American humour are poles apart. British humour is often introvert, snobbish, delighting in weird incongruity. American humour is brash, explosive, supersonic. Both races are reluctant to admit that the other has any sense of humour at all.

Leicestershire, property valued for probate in the United Kingdom. £1,000,000.[1]

A round figure.

The millionaire, Entwistle, is a fairly modern conception. It is stamped with its modernity and vulgarity. Fifty years ago people were classified in respect of their monetary standing in quite a different way.

You are determined

[1] Very rich men, these days, try to leave as little money as possible when they die, for obvious death-duty reasons, but human nature is reluctant to consider the inevitability of death so that they still get caught unawares with the odd million or so on their hands.

The majority, of course, were described as 'the poor'. They were considered to deserve charity for which, naturally, they had to be grateful. After the poor came those 'in comfortable circumstances'. This did not mean holidays on the Costa Brava, it meant that such people could, just, manage – in that state of life unto which it had pleased an omniscient Deity to call them. Above these happy folk were those who were, a little enviously perhaps, described as 'well off'. This might mean almost anything. For the British, the most cunning race on earth, often conceal their wealth. They did so in Queen Victoria's day. And they do so in Queen Elizabeth's day. They do it individually, and they do it collectively, as companies. This lets in the take-over bidder whom we will meet much later.

Further still up the ladder came the 'wealthy'. And, finally, that snug, serene coterie, 'the rich'.

I think it was the Americans who first simplified all this, making it factual and easy to understand. The American Press in fact invented the millionaire. The dollar millionaire that is. He represented a convenient milestone in a society devoted, as ours is, almost entirely to material objectives. Until the American male had achieved his million dollars he was on the way up. When he achieved it he had arrived. This was simple and satisfying. It has been complicated since by the advent of the multi-millionaire, people like Mr

Getty, the oil magnate; men who do not know just how many millions they have, but are quite sure that it is more than when the last account was taken.

Your last asset, Entwistle, is that you are in good health, and educated. That is to say you can read and write quite well, simple mathematics do not bother you. You have at least a smattering of general knowledge. The number of things you do not yet know, or are not sure about, is quite frightening.

You are in good health

You do not know when grouse and partridge shooting start and end.[1]

You do not know why a red hand is significant to a baronet.

Nineteen-o-six means nothing to you in connexion with port, and you do not even know the exact locality of the champagne district of France.

That is to say you are, technically, educated but socially ignorant. But this can be righted as we go along.

You'll do, Entwistle, for one reason only, that you are determined to become a millionaire, and a millionaire you will become.

Your disadvantages are manifest and manifold. You speak in an odd way, or in a way that sounds odd to me. Yes, I know, it may well be that I speak in a way that sounds odd to you. *Touché.* But the way I speak is the way that the British upper classes[2] (we are coming to them) and the B.B.C. speak, though there are minute, subtle differences between the two.

Do not worry or hurry about this matter of diction, just adapt your speech, year by year, to 'better' models.

[1] Grouse. August 12th to December 11th – the 10th in Scotland. Scots must be different.

Partridge. September 1st to February 2nd. As if you cared.

[2] The B.U.C.s may be a music-hall joke, but they have a healthy stranglehold in the City, on the Banks and on business everywhere. They keep their empire alive by constantly admitting successful newcomers. Don't worry about this. When you arrive we can fix you up – crest, coat of arms, the lot.

You may be told that it does not matter. Rubbish. It matters very much. If you retain, in all its raucous frightfulness, your full North Country – and Salford, ba gum – accent you will find it twice as hard to achieve your aim.

Looking down the list they will say:

'Ah, Entwistle. Yes, I know, competent, very competent. But a little on the rough side still? Never seems to have quite got off the factory floor, does he? Would the men respect him?'

And the answer will be, from the six yes-men round that table:

'You're dead right, Sir Walter. He'll have to wait. Mustn't let him go, though. Useful man. Knows the business inside out.'

Sir Walter says: 'We are agreed then, gentlemen. Young Playbright moves up. I must say your decision pleases me very much. The young man is my nephew, as you know. I am sure we shall be safe with him.'

Not what has really happened, Entwistle? You know more about this firm, the great steel Corporation of Gargantuan Steel, than young Mr Playbright will ever know. You know the technical side. You know the exact temperature of steel to make military swords, or good, stainless, Sheffield knives. You know the structure of the Corporation, its finance, its markets. You even have business vision, the rarest commodity of all. But you're not a 'gentleman'.[1]

It's very crude isn't it? You must become one.

You dress deplorably. Men's fashions in Britain, in spite of the *Tailor and Cutter*, never alter. They vacillate a little. Trousers are a little tighter, a little looser. An extra button goes – or comes back. But, by and large, your successful Englishman wears a certain kind of well-cut, macabre uniform that stamps him as what he is whether, at the moment, he happens to be in Belgrade, Bangkok, or Rio. I shall have to tell you how to dress, later.[2] Clothes make the man in England to a degree that no one cares to admit, and shoes, of course. They are a cult in themselves.[3]

Your manners are quite agreeable, but you are too aggressive. You need only to be determined. Underneath. Ruthless if you must,[4] but your manners could

[1] This term simply means a member of the B.U.C. Occasionally the word 'gentleman' is used in a wider, mystical sense. For instance when Rudyard Kipling, speaking of South Africa, wrote: 'English gentlemen, a few hotly to defend her,' he was using the word, I hope, in its wider connotation. In this sense it means a chivalrous fellow.

[2] For heaven's sake, Entwistle, if you must carry a pen, hide it in an inner pocket, do not parade it with pencils in a breast pocket. If you do, you will be regarded as an expert, or worse.

[3] Shoes are very significant. The very best shoes are neither blunt nor pointed, but have a lovely authoritative sleek appearance. Please do not tell me you cannot afford to have such shoes made for you. One of the first rules in the game of becoming a millionaire is to THINK RICH. Even before you become rich.

[4] The B.U.C. is ruthless. During the war a merchant was night-watching near a famous club. The members, warming to him, made him a member. After the war the little haberdasher unwisely asked one or

You are prepared to work yourself to death . . .

be greatly improved. In business you will need two manners. The first of a happily ingratiating variety, with a hint of genuflection, to be used towards your superiors, the second, which may be called authoritarian-camaraderie, for use towards those you have passed in the race. This manner is very useful. It leaves the recipients of its favours still your friends. You are still 'good old John' to them, but at the same time, from

two members to look him up for 'a sherry and a shirt'. He was promptly asked to resign. This type of disregard for the feelings of others is typical of the B.U.C.

18

your manner, from its occasional crispness, from its stark realism, they realize that you are going up, to the top, where, maybe, you'll remember them.

Yes, Entwistle, you'll do. You have inexhaustible ambition. You are prepared to work yourself to death. You will always be at work a little before the others, and often leave long after they have rejoined their television sets – and their curious little wives. But a few minutes of thought at this stage may save you a lot of trouble. There are two ways of becoming a millionaire. The old-fashioned hard way through working your way up every rung of the great grimy ladder of Gargantuan Steel until, in the end, you *are* Gargantuan Steel; and the modern, painless way by success in the world of high finance. This, too, needs guts, and brains, and work, but it also needs a rare gift of smell, so that you know in advance the odour of money. You know what makes shares rise, and what makes them fall. You need to be a gambler, too, but a cunning one. Either road, relentlessly followed, the road of commerce or the road of finance, will lead you to the promised land.

Which do you choose?

You choose Gargantuan Steel. How right you are. Stick to them. And when you have mastered the Corporation, perhaps a little financial exploitation? Why, yes, certainly. You have the right idea, Entwistle.

May I say a word about your religion and politics? I know, your faith is your own affair. But do not obtrude it. For some odd reason the City, which is not inexperienced, thinks that nonconformists are inclined to embezzle. There is still a prejudice against 'Roman' Catholics. And the British inner business circle frankly distrusts Jews.[1] You say you are a cool Christian. How

---

[1] Anti-Semitism is widely deplored in Britain (as in the States) and is only practised in its milder forms. For instance when a Jewish business man defaults the public say 'Ah!' in a most peculiar way. When a Gentile business man defaults a great many people say: 'Nice chap. Played table-tennis for his university. Sheer bad luck.'

... the same political convictions as you ...

very intelligent of you. You go to church at Christmas, Easter, for the Harvest Festival (can't resist the mammoth marrows) and on Armistice Day. Good show, Entwistle. Very good show, indeed.

Join the Tory Party. What is this you say? That you can't see any difference between the hydrogen-bomb diplomacy of Hugh Gaitskell and the hydrogen-bomb diplomacy of Rab Butler? No difference between the conservative Hugh as Chancellor, or the liberal Rab? Oh come, now, don't be difficult. You've been so good up to now. Believe me I do not ask you to join the Tories without reason. The Tory Party in England is more than a political party. It is the stamp of social and economic solidarity.

It's no good saying you have no politics in England. This is fatal. It's a Communist, undercover gambit. It's really no good saying that you reject the crass materialism of the Tory Party which has been so slavishly copied, in reverse, by the Socialists. It won't do. Join the Tories. Your life is going to be a gamble, however hard you work. In this one simple matter, play safe. Join the Tories. Live Tory, breathe Tory, eat Tory, drink Tory, smell Tory,[1] think Tory. You will? Thank God. Don't give me these shocks again.

One note of warning I must give you, Entwistle.

[1] It is not pukka to advertise, otherwise I would give you a list of the creams and lotions that procure this desirable result. They are very expensive, and unmistakable. You'll have to find this out for yourself.

There may come a time, halfway up the ladder, when the whole thing sickens you. You may say to yourself: What the hell am I working myself to death for?[1] I can't take it with me. I can go now and swim in the Blue Grotto from a villa in Capri. I can fly-fish, as I have always wanted to, on Devon rivers that tumble down from Dartmoor through sunlit gorges to the sea. What am I doing here, in the smog, working, working, working? One of ten million black beetles leading this ghastly pressurized life.

If that thought ever comes to you, banish it. Kill these visions.

And, finally, one day, if ever you have time to think – which is unlikely – you may say to yourself: Isn't the whole system mad? This crazy, competitive rat-race? It's lunatic. We have enough gold, and diamonds, and wheat, and rice, and fruit, and water, for everyone. All we need to do is to plan a non-competitive economy on a world basis. We have enough gas, and electricity, and even nuclear power. We don't all have to cut each other's throats. We have passed out of the Age of Want into the Age of Plenty, but we cannot realize our good fortune.

I am sorry, Entwistle, I must stamp on these dangerous whimsies right away. You are running with the rats,

[1] Ninety per cent of would-be millionaires worry. This leads to a hypersensitive condition or thrombosis. Very few observe reasonable rules of sleep and diet. Simplicity is alien to them.

23

my boy, and if you jump out of line they will turn and eat you. The whole ghastly, wasteful pretence of the money God is at stake. The Romans did not worship Money in the Temple of Juno for nothing. We worship it in every Church, every council, every office of the land. The Lord, thy God, is a jealous God. . . .

Accept the rules. Accept the code. Gird yourself, Entwistle. It's a great and glittering prize that you wish to win. You must work like a beaver, and be as wise as a serpent – for there are traps on the way.

2

THE OFFICE

IT IS here, in this office, Entwistle, that you will make your name. Even if, in the first instance, you have joined Gargantuan Steel as a sales representative, it is by your periodic appearances at the office that you will be judged.

It depends entirely upon the image of you that people have in their minds whether you will climb the ladder slowly, painfully, or with a rapidity that will surprise – and appal – your friends. It is up to you to make that image strong, self-reliant, and reasonably efficient. This is as far as you can go. It may well be that the whole structure of Gargantuan Steel needs drastic overhaul, that it is Victorian in its production and sales methods, but, for the present, you had better keep your remedies to yourself. There are thousands of businesses running profitably in Britain today on inefficient lines. The Directors do not want to alter course. Eventually, of course, changing conditions and new markets will betray the weakness, but you should not expose it. If they are forced to ask for guidance they will do so. You can then produce the mental blue-print which you have tactfully harboured all these years. They will not be grateful, but they will be impressed. They will be in your debt.

At the moment your personal relationships in the office are what really matter. To get on well with people – and that is your object – you must be sensitive enough to realize that office personalities are always only one side of a man's or a woman's character.

Take Beacher, the Area Sales Manager. Stout, forty-one. Apt to drink slightly too much. Testy. Not an easy boss.

Beacher acts in the way he does because two factors, hidden from the office, have shaped his life. The first is that during the war he obtained a temporary commission in the Brigade of Guards and he hates being in Gargantuan Steel after being a major in a good regiment. The second influence is his wife. She is not a nagger. She is something much worse. She is a whiner. She whines, day and night.

This gives Beacher an acute feeling of frustration and inferiority. He has not the guts to have a showdown with his wife who is irritatingly efficient in the home.

You must not knuckle under to Beacher. He will bully you if he can. But you should realize that you can do more for this man than he can do for you. What Beacher needs is confidence and courage. You should have these qualities, for they are the handmaidens of ambition.

Perhaps the surest test of your calibre is how you deal with the secretary problem, when you reach a position where you have a secretary. If she is plain and efficient no real problem presents itself. If, as so often happens, she has been chosen as much for her looks as for her capability, the matter is more complex. It is impossible to leave out of your calculations entirely the fact that she is a girl and you are a man. Moreover she is the girl you will see much more of than any other woman, except your wife.

I know an exceptionally able London executive who for years now has had a charming and efficient secretary. She married and had a child, but continued to work. She is there today, looking as lovely as ever, and, I am told, more capable than she has ever been. She is devoted to her boss. He calls her Faith. She calls him Mr Wallace in the office, and Charles outside. Recently I asked him how it was done.

'It is very simple. For five years now, that is since she has worked for me, I have put a rose on her desk every Monday morning. She loves flowers. I have plenty in my garden. Apart from this I stick to my guns, and I expect and get complete co-operation.'

Although your manner to those under you is important, your manner to those above is vital. Forthrightness, charming deference, even flicks of humour, all these can be used. For there are but two means of locomotion to the top. Either people must like you so much that they push you there, or you, yourself, are so good that you push yourself there. The two methods are not exclusive, but can be very happily combined.

The crucial test in the office will be, not your relationships, but your knowledge and industry. Mr Roy Thomson the tough, genial, extrovert Tsar of the ex-Kemsley Empire was asked why he thought some broke through to great wealth while others, equally endowed, could not do so. His answer is a classic:

'I guess they just don't want money enough.'

Mr. Thomson, whose favourite reading is balance sheets, wanted money very much indeed. After conquering Canada he subdued Scotland, and now London has fallen to him. Why? Very little education. 'We were too poor,' he says. No great charm. No imposing appearance. One thing only, an implacable determination to become a rich man. And absolute conviction that money is another word for success. 'If you don't make money you're a failure aren't you? If you make it you're a success.'

Is it possible to win complete success without adopting this philosophy? It is very difficult, but may not be impossible. For here you are up against a real difficulty, a barrier of the spirit. We know that Mr Thomson's philosophy of life is basically false. Success does not consist in making money. It consists in achieving real happiness for yourself and others. So the question has to be put: Can you become a millionaire – and remain healthy and happy? Yes, I think that could be done, too, though it very seldom is. You would have to have a philosophy that enabled you to see the race for wealth in its true perspective. You could run the race to the last ounce of your strength, and skill, and courage, and still remain the master of your own spirit. But if you could do that you would be very much more than a millionaire. You would be, in your way, a great man.

Part of your office impact will be made by personal relationships, but partly it will be made on paper. It is essential that, from the start, you should be able to write a good business letter. This means:

1. That the gist of the letter is tackled in the opening lines.

2. That business clichés, the hallmark of the second-rate, are avoided.

3. That the meaning should be clear beyond shadow of doubt.

4. That the general impression should be cordial.

Entwistle, read the very best letters and minutes. Not, of necessity, from business sources. Read Sir Winston Churchill's minutes. Read the reports of the Chairmen of the five great Banks. Study style. It will stand you in good stead. For the level of business correspondence in Britain is deplorably low. British business men, it seems, do not really believe in letters. The Americans make no such mistake. They realize that the letter is an extension of the firm reaching out to Moscow, or Paris, or Shanghai. They take endless trouble in composing a pleasing letter on fine notepaper. Take this hint. There is no more powerful method of communication than the letter-box.[1]

If you become, by practice, a writer of fine business letters, you should be equally good on the telephone. The telephone is a dangerous instrument. You never know, from one moment to the next, who is going to enter your life through its medium. So be circumspect

[1] Books have been written on how to write the perfect business letter, but, in fact, there are very few basic rules that ensure that your letters will be models of their kind. Here are the chief pointers:

1. Use the simplest language possible and avoid all clichés like the plague.

2. Express the whole thing and the sole thing. Get to grips with your subject at once and in the clearest terms.

3. Never abbreviate.

4. Use complete courtesy always. Even when collecting debts from reluctant debtors.

5. If you are corresponding with titles or honours, get them absolutely correct.

6. Let your firm have excellent business writing-paper. Cheap paper is the worst possible economy. The paper is your herald.

31

with the telephone. Courtesy costs nothing, but may pay surprising dividends. The petty business mogul who snaps and barks on the phone is his own confession of mediocrity.

What you will really be judged by, in the long run, is your loyalty and knowledge. As long as you are with Gargantuan Steel they deserve your loyalty. For better or for worse. Ill used or well treated, you owe them allegiance. There may come a time when you have to leave them. The road ahead may be too congested in the Corporation. Too many young Playbrights may be cluttering up the Board. A great rival firm may offer you a job on a higher level, with the way clear. Then you must take it. The tide in the affairs of men comes, but, often, it only comes once. Hesitation at that point of your career would be fatal. You may even come back to Gargantuan Steel one day as . . . well very high up in the hierarchy.

Your knowledge should extend far beyond the office. You must know steel inside out. Steel in America, steel in Germany, steel in Japan. You must know steel in all its colours – faint yellow, straw yellow, brownish yellow, purple spots, purple, pale blue, dark blue, black blue. You must know the steel prices day by day and the annual trends and fluctuations. You must know something of the steel Trade Unions and strikes. There is no aspect of steel of which you can afford to be ignorant. All this knowledge, painfully acquired, may not be of use for years, but one day you will need it. It is this that will mark you out from the hundred other young executives in Gargantuan Steel when promotion day at last comes round.

Before very long the powers that be will see to it that you are moved to Head Office. And this is your chance. For here Sir Walter works – and he is the Alpha and Omega of Gargantuan Steel. And Sir Walter is no fool. Though he may be willing to push his nephew, young Playbright, on to the Board, he knows that nepotism can be death in a competitive market. So he has an eye on you. The last time your name cropped up there was a murmur from his yes-men that, though you would have to wait, on no account should they let you go. Because you knew the business inside out. Sir Walter never forgot that. At the back of his mind is an unseen memo and on it is written the one word 'Entwistle'.

He may feel now that the time is coming when you should take a big step forward, but he is still worried about your 'authority'. So, out of the blue, he asks you to dinner. With your wife, of course. And you accept. It is a command. It is your first visit to his house. You know you are going to be vetted, tested, and it is an ordeal. There is only one way to meet it – to be entirely natural.

c   33

at the back of
his mind is an
unseen memo

(It may well be worth your while to study Sir Walter's hobbies.
You find he is interested in Chinese porcelain? Good. He specializes in
famille rose? Excellent. Learn all you need to know about famille-rose
china with its characteristic peony. And learn a little more than you have
to. Know about 'famille noire' and 'famille verte' as well – and about
Oriental Lowestoft which can look so like famille rose. If you are able to
spot a piece of Oriental Lowestoft that Sir Walter, bless him, thought
was famille rose, his opinion of you will soar. He will never forget it.)

34

3

THE FIRST TEN THOUSAND

You must look into this question of money and capital very carefully, Entwistle, for in the immediate future you must lay your hands on a substantial sum of money, your first capital. As soon as you have got this money you will be able to acquire a great deal more, but without it your attempts will be met with frustration and defeat. You will have to fall back on saving, which is slow and painful – but not to be despised.

When you have a good round sum, say ten thousand pounds, you can go to your Bank Manager and say: 'I have a venture which I want to pursue. Here are the figures. It will cost at least a hundred thousand pounds, but we estimate the profit, in one year, at not less than thirty thousand. The figures speak for themselves.'

And your Bank Manager, tilting his spectacles, will give you a shrewd, hard look and say:

'How much are you investing in this project, Mr Entwistle?'

Now, if you can reply: 'Ten thousand pounds, my entire capital,' the Bank will consider all aspects of your proposal very carefully. They may even have information that you do not possess – they are very well informed – and may be able to help you in your plans. In any case they will investigate your proposal carefully. If, with suitable precautions to cover themselves, they decide to back you, you have a powerful experienced ally. You are on the road.

But if you go to your Bank with a similar project, before you have acquired any capital, the answer is likely to be:

'This is not the type of business we care to do. We are bankers, not speculative financiers.' Quite right, too, for they are thinking: 'This man is risking nothing himself.'

So your problem is to acquire, honestly, your initial capital.

It will not do you any harm, Entwistle, to know the history of money, the story of gold and silver. It is a strange and fascinating tale. You will, for instance, discover that in old China the Haikwan tael was equal to ten mace, which was equal to a hundred candareens, which was equal to a thousand 'cash'. You will learn that there were no national gold or silver coins in China, but that Mexican dollars were highly valued and widely exchanged, while foreign coins were accepted at their weight value.

This erudition may not be a waste of time. I had an intelligent, inquisitive friend who turned his knowledge of Mexican dollars to good use. He found that they were very convenient if regarded as bullion in gold deals. He was then a Bangkok business man. He is now a financier dealing in world currencies with an office – need I tell you? – in Switzerland; Zurich to be exact, where they have those discreet international banking accounts with no names.

Let me tell you how he did it. Immediately after the last war the American market was crying out, at a high price, for Siamese zircons, the gay garish little semi-precious stone of Siam that looks so like a diamond in the dimmed lights of a nightclub. At the same time the market in Macao was screaming for gold. My friend, a thoughtful type, said to himself: 'We have a marriage here.' He bought zircons cheaply in Bangkok with

keep your ear
to the ground

ticals, the local currency. He flew them by air, well insured, to New York and sold them very profitably for good American dollars. With these good American dollars he bought Mexican dollars and flew them to Bangkok and Macao. He sold the gold – at a handsome profit. Yes, he was quite willing to be paid in ticals, with which he bought zircons.[1]

I think you will agree that a man with this amount of practical vision deserved to become a financier in Zurich. Now he knows every permutation of the franc, the mark, the lira, the dollar, and the pound, and he

[1] The present paper tical replaced the silver coin which, in its turn, replaced the silver-button tical.

still keeps a loving eye on Far Eastern currencies, and financial gaps.

For you, Entwistle, such glamorous possibilities and opportunities may not present themselves. To get your start you will need good information, and good friends. The friends may include your relatives. If you are really on to a good thing, and can demonstrate this, you will find you have backers where you never suspected. But first obtain your project.

Keep your eyes and ears open. All information is legitimate except that which you obtain through Gargantuan Steel. You must never cross your lines.

For instance it is general knowledge that Mammoth, the German Steel giant, is setting up business in Britain, anxious to acquire steel-processing firms in conjunction with its own great production works.

What Mammoth are going to do, my boy, is to buy up, as cheaply as possible, the small steel-processing and steel-product firms that are conveniently near their own great new site outside Birmingham.

Clear yourself with Gargantuan first. They are not interested? Good. The field is clear.

You cannot do the business you have in mind, yourself, Entwistle. It is too big for you. You have to have an associate – and friend. How about Leon Bull, the very smart young broker you played golf with on Saturday? Leon was friendly. Obviously he liked you.

He would not have told you all those excruciatingly funny stories if he had not done so. You know, instinctively, that Leon will not betray a trust. He will be a clam in confidential business. That is enough.

Leon, it is clear, is a very lively customer. He's out to become a millionaire, too – and no lingering. So approach him quietly, and privately.

'Leon' – it's Leon and John now – 'Leon, I think that Mammoth are going to buy the small steelworks for

Obviously he liked you.

twenty miles around their new plant. I lunched with Hardacre on Wednesday. He's a Salford man, where I come from. His brother works in Birmingham. Has just joined Mammoth . . . I have checked. The information is accurate. Anyone who could get in quick might make a nice killing.'

For a moment there is silence. Leon's brain is summing up, very fast, the import of your uncasual remark.

Then he smiles. 'Right. We buy in my name before Mammoth get around to it. Sell out to Mammoth. Split fifty-fifty. How much have you got?'

Now you have scraped the till, your own family till plus a loan from a friend. No need to tell Leon this.

'Practically nothing. Three hundred, perhaps.'

Leon blinks at this. 'Never mind. I'll put up the necessary balance. The information was all yours. Most of the money will be mine. If the Bank will back us we might go to a hundred thousand. Is there a small firm in the area we can buy for that?'

'Hemming Brothers. Bolts, flanges,[1] and hinges. Been a bit rocky since the depression. George Hemming – he's the senior partner – wants to get out. Wants to live in Capri – his wife has a cancer. . . .'

---

[1] Mr Justice Rigby Swift once asked Counsel in a commercial case: 'What is a flange?' He then turned to the Jury and said: 'This is not judicial ignorance. I know exactly what a flange is. But I thought that one or two of you might not know.' He was quite right. They didn't.

'We'll buy Hemmings. Leave it to me. Might get it for eighty thousand – cash.'

The project is launched, conceived in the minds of Leon and yourself, and the wheels are now turning.

Leon will play it very cool. Very cool indeed. George Hemming is secretly so excited by the liberation he sees ahead that, very reluctantly, he accepts Leon's offer of seventy-six thousand pounds in cash for a controlling interest in the old-established firm of Hemming Brothers, the firm founded by his grandfather, 'Old George', way back in 1851 when the world was young and muck meant money.

And you, Entwistle? How do you feel? You have parted with all your savings, if we may call them that. They are in Leon's supple hands. You have to trust Leon. You have to take the business risks involved in this enterprise. If your information is correct, Mammoth will be bidding for Hemmings in the months to come. You wait. At last a move is made. Mammoth approach the Hemming Directors. The Managing Director is still a Hemming, though George Hemming has gone off to Capri with that poor wife of his. Mammoth are surprised to discover that a Mr Leon Bull, a young broker, has a controlling interest in Hemmings, but they want this firm. They pounce. Eighty thousand? No. A hundred thousand, says Mr Hemming – after

42

You are nineteen thousand pounds richer.

consultation with Leon. Ninety? No. Ninety-five, then?
. . . Pause. Very well, ninety-five it is.

Leon and you, Entwistle, have cleared nineteen
thousand pounds by information, daring, and courage.
Leon asks you, quite casually, as you play golf, how
would you like your slice paid?

In cash? By cheque? No. Let Leon acquire good
shares for you. The market is rising. On these shares,
in your name now, you can acquire money for future
ventures.

You and Leon have made your first killing. Clever
young men. Anyone else, with the knowledge, could
have done it, but you did it. You risked your savings.
You trusted Leon. You might have been stuck with
Hemmings. Instead your plan, an intelligent plan of
anticipation, worked out as you foresaw. Where there
is no vision, business wanes, but, where there is vision,
it waxes.

For the Lord's sake, Entwistle, keep quiet about this
coup. It's capital gain, not income. No need to tell
the income-tax people. The income tax from your
newly acquired shares in Argentine Beef, Rand Gold,
and Amalgamated (London) Properties will be de-
ducted at source. Carry on as if the world had not
changed for you.

In fact, of course, the world has changed for you.
Wider horizons beckon. You are capitalists now, you

and Leon – you had better stick together in your mutual interest.

You move in an ever-widening circle, meet old friends from Lancashire. You hear that the row of houses in Salford where you lived is up for sale. No buyers. How about you and Leon moving in – at a price? Conversion. Flats. The Bank again. They have confidence now. They know that you and Leon honour your obligations to the minute.

Remember, Entwistle, that the best money is often under your nose. That tumbledown skating-rink where you used to enjoy yourself as a kid? It's going cheap. Buy it, renovate it, advertise it, sell it.

And when you move in to buy a business insist that you have an option on some of the shares. If your brains are going to create profits where none were before, you should be the one to benefit. Keep faith with Leon, and those who lend you money, always. Then money will always be available. Let one man down, and the river of gold will dry up overnight.

It happens that sometimes people have information and do not act on it.

Take elections. The newspaper forecasts are very accurate. They know. So you know, too, who is going to win. But – it hasn't happened yet. The public hold back until they know the result – too late. You and Leon can act on the forecasts. You know how the share market will react. Have the courage of other people's statistics.

So, as opportunity after opportunity unfolds itself, the familiar phrase will be:

'Leon, old boy, we'd better get cracking.'

You will have your reverses. But you will ride the storms, for you and Leon deserve to win. Intelligent. Informed. Energetic. Two young men in the swim. In the fashion, too. For money is the new God. Even the Church kneels down and worships it, clearing three millions on property deals in a year. Good luck to them. It will help them raise the wages of the many good and hardworking men in the Ministry.

Do not rush to change your mode of living. You can take holidays abroad now, as Leon has always done. You can taste the bitter-sweet tang of France, the blood of the Spanish bull-rings, the lure that is Italy.

Don't let it go to your head. When you meet your old friends, remember them. You're going to be very rich, Entwistle, no need to let the gold corrode your soul.

4

SUITS AND A CAR

Now that fortune beckons, Entwistle, you will have to change your habits. It's the saloon bar for you from now on, and you pay a penny a pint more with good grace.

This is, in a quiet, subdued British way, a dramatic turning point in your career. You are leaving the working class and joining the bosses. You are moving out of the lower classes and joining the middle class. You have a long way to go before you join the upper and governing class, but this is change enough for the time being.

May we start by burning those deplorable ready-made suits of yours? I know that there is years of wear in them yet. Give them to brother George, but be rid of them at all costs. You need a tailor now.

I deplore the fact that you must change your habits but there is no way out. The British people cling to their class shackles with a fanatical devotion. They do not want equality. They spit on it whenever given the chance to do so, politically and socially. The

47

hierarchy must be maintained and each layer must have its personal habits, label, and name.

So you have to have a tailor. There are perhaps ten first-class tailors in London. They are not all in Savile Row. But they all have the same peculiarities. They like to be introduced to people before they serve them. You can't go in and smack down your forty guineas and say: 'Give us a suit.' You can have a suit slowly and deliberately built for you and then, perhaps

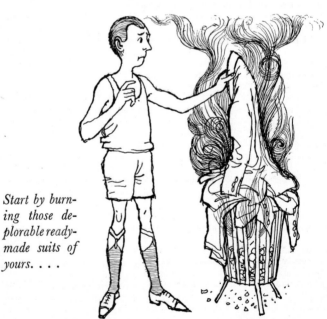

Start by burning those deplorable ready-made suits of yours. . . .

six months later, you may write a cheque for the bill. Please do not carry any cash with you on your first visit. It will damn you. The upper tailory detest cash. They regard it as an insult.[1]

The suits that these people will make for you are so good that tailors in America and China will take a London suit to pieces just to learn the magic of the craft.[2] And these suits will last you ten or twenty years – if you keep your figure by jumpology.

Tailors, you will find, are very touchy at present, chiefly because they have no recognized leader of fashion to inspire them. Prince Philip just does not seem to take an interest in clothes. He is the kind of man who disdains to wear a hat, could not care less what length his trousers are, and, except in uniform, has a swaggering, swashbuckling, damn-it-any-old-thing-will-do attitude towards his clothes. This distresses the upper tailory very much. True the Duke of Kent 'conforms', but it's not quite the same thing. The tailors sigh for the good old days of Edward VII. When this merry Monarch said that black shoes might be

[1] London tailors are actually insulted by the offer of cash. A racing man, pressed by his tailor for payment of something on account, pulled a wad of notes from his pocket and paid his bill in full. The reply was: 'This is most unusual. We hope you will take your custom elsewhere.'

[2] London tailors really are the best in the world. Neither Paris nor Washington can touch them. For his 1960 State visit to Britain the King of Siam ordered five thousand pounds worth of suits and uniforms from Prince Philip's tailor. The tailor and the cutter flew the seven thousand miles to Bangkok for fittings.

worn even with a brown suit – but not of course vice-versa – that was that. His son, the sailor King, would wear the crease on his trousers from side to side instead of from front to back, and this again was divine authority. The tailors followed the fashion with a happy bleat. Even as recently as Edward VIII, the Prince of Wales that was, though he loved novelty, at least he loved fashion too. He wasn't a damned sceptic like some people we know.

The danger of Prince Philip from the tailor's point of view is that he may pass on his ideas of harum-scarum dressing to the present Prince of Wales. That would be too awful, and the London tailors pray nightly that young Charles will be a fashionable young man, a credit to his tailor.

I mention these matters, Entwistle, because I want you to realize the kind of people these tailors are. It will probably take you a year or so before the firm really know your name and recognize you, but once they have so to speak decided to adopt you, they will follow your career with interest. They will know everything you do. Your successes will be their joy. They will never forget you. You will have to stay with them to the end of the road. It may be possible to change tailors in London, but no one has yet discovered how this can be done without disrupting the smooth working of the unwritten British Constitution.

One or two trifling points you must bear in mind. The buttons on your coat sleeve must be real and they must go in and out of real buttonholes. Your handkerchief must be mashed into your pocket anyhow, not poked in cleverly as actors are wont to do. I beg you to take advice on ties. You do not have old-school ties. That is a blessing. They will fix you up with some beautifully restrained shirts and ties that will be instantly recognizable by those who know.

Your successes will be their joy

Your shoemaker will be almost as reluctant and as aloof as your tailor at first, but he too will get to know you as the years pass by. You know, of course, Entwistle, that England would never be the same again if the very best shoes were not polished underneath, between the sole and the heel, as well as on top? I only mention it. This absolute must recently led Scotland Yard to the arrest of an upper-crust criminal.

They knew, Entwistle. You must know, too.

And then, of course, there is the crucial matter of a car. Certain makes are out as far as you are concerned. All the popular cars are taboo. Fords are untouchable. Austins are beyond the pale. The Morris is unmentionable. Your safest bet is a Singer or a Rover. Colour, grey or beige. Beige is the rage in Britain and has been for the last fifty years. Women dress in all shades of brown and biscuit. It hides their sex. Horses are nearly always beige whether the experts call them chestnut or just brown. Most English flowers are beige. And the British rivers, teeming with trout, a beige fish, are beige, too. You get the point. A good brownish Rover.

You can have foreign club insignia so long as they are in metal, preferably silver, but no foreign paper labels. This is a family car and the whole point of it is that it should be inconspicuous yet comfortable. Not flashy. Not, for heaven's sake, multicoloured like these

ghastly American atrocities. Just a good, dull mono-
chrome. British, beige. You are very quick, Entwistle.
I see you have already caught the essential spirit of the
middle-class car.

That's another hurdle passed.

You may think that in this modern age it does not
matter a damn how you dress or what type of car you
drive. You are wrong. There is a deep and good reason
for its importance in the British character and habits.
The basic British conception of public and business
life is that power should never be exercised by the men
who really know – the experts.

Fatuous, you say? Not at all. The British people
have decided that experts are often fanatics with limited
vision. They hate fanatics. That is why they were able
to mobilize five hundred million people to defeat Hitler.
Perhaps they carry their conviction too far. The
amateur is the English ideal, the balanced, genial
amateur with an open mind.

The rule applies to every section of public activity.
The politicians? All or nearly all amateurs. Certainly
the Cabinet and the Shadow Cabinet (for the Labour
Party clings to the old routine with desperate conserva-
tism under the arch Tory, Mr Hugh Gaitskell) are
entirely composed of amateurs.

At the moment we have an ex-Don in charge of the
Police, and a pig-farmer in charge of education. Good

show. They cannot possibly know too much about it.

The Army and the Navy are run by professionals – up to the top, but not at the top. In the English estimation it requires a country gentleman, or a Company Director, to run the Navy and the Army as they should be run. And the Air Force, too, must never be run by a serving officer, however distinguished.

Now we have carried this rule into business. You, Entwistle, are about to become a Director of Gargantuan Steel. You must join the ranks of the amateurs. By your behaviour, by your speech, by your manners, by your clothes and house, you must make it plain that steel is not your only interest. It may still absorb you, but it must no longer engulf you.

You must slowly pattern yourself on the men who run British business, and they are a bunch of golfers, hunters, philatelists, gardeners, fly-fishers, and yachtsmen.[1]

You must now groom yourself for complete amateur status. It is quite easy for you to test if what I say is true. Look at the five great Banks. Who is the boss? A banker? Not on your life! Who are the Company

[1] A very successful broker and business man often has his 'conferences' interrupted by his wife ringing up to give him details of the private lives of their prize-winning herd of pigs. Asked whether this did not interfere with business, he replied: 'Certainly not. The British like and trust a man who can break off a deal to listen to the ailments of a famous sow.'

... the men who run British business...

Directors of the City of London? The men at the very top? They are squires in Dorset, farmers in Norfolk, landowners in Leicestershire. They are amateurs to a man.

There are a hundred and one smaller points that you must attend to as you await the big rise. Have you any calling cards? Yes? Let me look at them. My God,

Entwistle, how could you? These cards are printed. . . .
Get rid of them this minute. Never let one be seen again.
Go to a good engraver and have your cards suitably
engraved. The shining black print will stand out like a
thin black vein from the exquisite white of the card itself.
These you may use with assurance. Those that you are
now throwing away would have betrayed you silently.

A little thing, a card. But British life is made up of
significant trifles. The Chinese – who in their cunning,
honesty, and mastery of alcohol so closely resemble
the British – immediately recognized the importance
of cards when they were introduced from the West.
The Chinese had a type of card of their own, but this
was half passport, half social credential. The modern
European calling card was introduced into China by
the Old China Hands a hundred years ago. They took
it to China with their furniture, their China, their
wine, their dogs, their wives, and their British superi-
ority. As soon as the Chinese saw the cards used as a
social introduction they knew they were on to something. At first the big men had big cards to show how
big they were. But it was not very long before the
Chinese caught the refinements of the British idea. The
very biggest men – the right-hand men of the Empress,
the Governors of vast provinces – had minute, delicately
engraved cards made for themselves.

The victory of the second basic rule of British public

life – that the bigger you are the quieter and nicer you are – was complete.

And it is to this second rule of life in the United Kingdom that I must now draw your attention, Entwistle.

The British hate ostentation. Only on great occasions do they permit display, but when they do they do

the British hate ostentation

it very well, calling on the pages of history to speak for them. Apart from this, apparent modesty is taken as a sign of strength. And of Authority. You may be able to find the High Court in London and even the Court of Appeal, but if you can find the Supreme Court of Appeal for the British Empire, called, foxily, and with typical misleading modesty, 'the Judicial Committee of the Privy Council', you're a better man than I am, Entwistle.[1]

To complete your rounded social picture, as you join the Board of Gargantuan Steel, you should have a club, Entwistle – a London club. It will cost you between ten and fifty guineas a year, but from your point of view it's worth it.

There is every type of club in London for you to choose from, but I suggest the Junior Conservative. You remember I was very firm about you joining the Tory Party. The Junior Conservative has good food, good drink, a membership of upper-crust business men and a very few members of the professions and the arts (discouraged). Sometimes on a Sunday morning the Prime Minister may drop in for a sherry, very dry, just to 'keep in touch' and to show what a simple fellow he still is, and that his ducal connexions haven't gone to his head in the least.

[1] Several great London businesses pride themselves on having small, inconspicuous premises and *never* advertising. The most famous hatter in London is a brilliant example of this.

When he does this a little informal circle will gather round him. You may join them. You are at the apex of power politics – and business – in Britain. For the Tory Party – do not forget – is the servant of big business as surely as the Labour Party, for all its independent posturing, is the servant of the Trade Unions.

Yes, the Junior Conservative will make a pleasing addition to your visiting card.

You are now almost ready, Entwistle. Ready for the invitation that will mean the first great step towards the realization of your ambition. A letter from Sir Walter:

> 'My dear Entwistle,
>
>   At our meeting on Wednesday my colleagues and I unanimously decided to invite you to join us on the Board of Directors of Gargantuan Steel. . . .'

It is the first accolade.

5

THE LITTLE WOMAN

WE HAVE assumed, my dear Entwistle, that you are married, but if you have not already taken this formidable and unpredictable plunge may I give you some words of advice on choosing your mate.

She should be English, or Scottish, not Welsh or Irish, for these outer lands are better married to their own men so that they can carouse, and sing, and cry together understandingly. The only foreign countries you may choose from are America, which includes the United States, as well as British America; and France. I do not know why this is. It is just so. It may well be that Brazilian, Rumanian, and Greek girls make lovely and efficient wives, but the British business world suspects them. If at a City dinner of the Worshipful Company of Cutlers you say: 'My wife is Spanish,' this immediately suggests to your audience a flamboyant, flashing-eyed beauty with a red rose in her mouth, who, at the drop of a kerchief, would give away the firm's secret projects. But if you can proudly say: 'My wife is Scottish, or British, or Canadian,' the impression

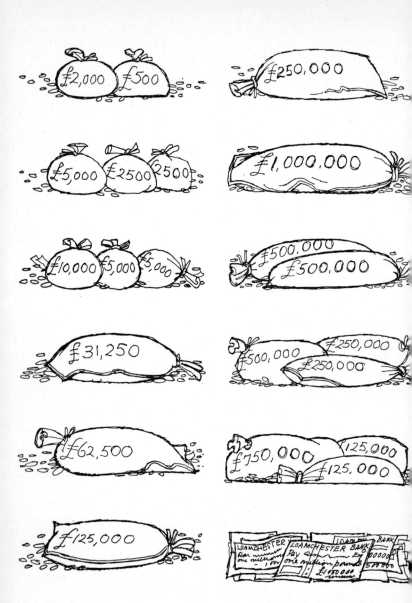

is one of steadfast loyalty, of tact, discretion, everything a young executive could desire. I do not know
why the French are included in possible wives for up-
and-coming British business men, but they are. There
is a theory that all the men who control the business
destinies of Britain have so long ago surrendered to the
charm of French women that there is one of those
secret, almost mystical, British conspiracies to let all
French ladies in, as it were, on the ground floor. Per-
sonally I favour this theory and believe it would stand
up to the closest inspection.

All oddities – Ethiopians and actresses – are defi-
nitely out. I do not know why actresses should be taboo.
When they do marry important men they often make
a great success of it, but the City, which is eighteenth
century in its approach to these subjects, regards women
who have been on the stage as gay seducers of mankind
not to be regarded seriously for the matrimonial stakes.

So there you are. Better buy British. You may, of
course, already have married Helen, the girl next
door. In which case she will adapt herself to your
changed circumstances at least as quickly as you are
able to do. But if you have not done this, the surest bet
to procure business and social advancement, which is
all tied up with your million pounds, is to marry a
horsy wife. She need not be what is known in the odd
jargon of English snobbery, as 'county'. But she must

be able to talk about horses. The type of horse does not really matter – the hunter, the show-jumper, the hack, whatever it is, it is acceptable.

All your co-Directors, though they may not know a fetlock from an off-fore, will appreciate your wife's horsy talk enormously. It will make them feel secure. They will come back at her with incredibly boring tales of their private lives – their salmon-fishing in Norway, their rough shooting in Devon, their square-rigged barque, the *Ursula* – wonderful in a cross-wind tacking to starboard. And the higher up in Society you progress the better will she be appreciated. Should you ever be asked to tea at the very top, a sigh of relief will go up when they realize that she understands about horses too – even about polo ponies, too good to be true.

Right, you have the first essential. Now what type of wife should you choose? Should you look for your fate in Chelsea where the young women are apt to know too much, or in North Devon where they say: 'Do come in. Mummy is out, but I'll make you some tea'?

What you do not want to do is to marry the young woman from North Devon and then get so bored with her that you have the young woman from Chelsea as your second or unofficial wife.

This is absolutely not done, or if it is it is very, very

naughty. Britain is the most monogamous nation on earth. It is not yet a matriarchy as the United States is, but the idea of one wife, one man is deeply entrenched. Even our worldly old archbishops are united on this. No polygamy. True, it is natural for a man to have more than one woman, but in business circles, at any rate, it is most undesirable. There is a relaxation of the rule on holidays. It is generally accepted that Directors who have to go abroad, on business or pleasure, may have temporary wives in the countries they are visiting, so long as the loved one does not turn up in London. What you must not do is to have a car accident with a heading in the *Daily Scoop* saying: 'Young British Director in Crash' and announcing to the world at large that: 'Mr John Entwistle, a British business man, and his charming companion, Madame Midinette Madalade, the film producer [inset], were involved in a car accident on the N7 near Cannes yesterday. . . .' Nor must Madame send a telegram to your wife assuring her that 'John is all right'.

Better play safe, Entwistle, and marry a nice, fresh, strong, frank, cheery girl from the country, who loves you. I had almost forgotten that. Cynical we may be, but no one will ever persuade us that loyalty is not the only quality in marriage that really counts. In the exciting days of 1940 a fighter squadron in Britain asked to name the first quality they looked for in

E

marriage gave the same answer. After that came domesticity, attraction, humour, and health in that order. Wise as well as brave young men.

Once married, of course, you must be the boss. Women hate ruling their men, but they will do so at the drop of a hat. In case you do not already know it, what women appreciate is a judicious mixture of brutality and tenderness. They must always fear with a delicious dread that you might beat them if they really misbehaved. But at the same time the little endearments that cost nothing at all mean a great deal to these odd, calculating, passionate, unpredictable creatures.

Do not kid yourself, Entwistle, that your wife will have a brain as men understand it. Logic is anathema to women. Words are suspect, too. It is never any good saying to the little woman: 'Let's talk this over quietly.' That is exactly what she has no intention of doing. She either wants to scream or laugh. She does not want your fatuous logic. But she is very easily diverted. For all women are frivolous if given half a chance. They are the hunted enchantresses. They can seduce and captivate and love. So, for the Lord's sake, do not try to reason with them.

When I say, and I do say, without fear of serious contradiction, that women have no brain in the usually accepted meaning of the word, I do not mean that they cannot arrive very quickly at excellent conclusions. They can, but they do it by a combination of insight and instinct that cannot possibly be described as thought – or any form of mental process. Their quasi-animal divinations are faster than logic, often more accurate than the reasoned conclusion. That is why they are so devastating. This applies in particular to any suggestion that there may be even the slightest warmth of feeling between you and another woman. When there is no evidence of this whatever, but it just happens to exist, your wife will smell it out with the unerring infallibility of a Maori witch-doctor. Bear all this in mind, Entwistle, when you are choosing your mate, and after you have chosen her.

Your wife, I need hardly say, will have the same political convictions that you have. Women, except a few entertaining freaks, are not interested in politics. Decades ago, at the time of the suffragette movement, a few abnormal women persuaded Britain that there was going to be a great and good 'Women's Vote for Peace, and Fairness, and the Home' when women got the vote. It was all a myth. Women have now had the vote for forty years – and done nothing with it whatever – following their husbands blindly when playing what they regard as a mildly foolish male game. Knowing this, you have the right to insist that the little woman votes Tory too. After all, the Trade Unions bully people into voting Labour. Why should you not exercise your *droits de Seigneur*?

One thing you must never allow your wife to do. She must never let you down in public.

If you are able truly to love her, she will repay you with dividends of devotion that make those property-share hand-outs look mean.

So marry, Entwistle, wisely – and once.

6

BLOOD SPORTS AND THE CHILDREN

THE British are an earthy race. They spring from the good earth of Britain and, as soon as finances permit, they return to it. Let me explain. It is the ambition of men on their way to becoming millionaires, and those who have accumulated millions, to become English country gentlemen and farmers. The farmer part has a special – financial tax – significance which I will dissect for you later, but the country-gentleman part is quite distinct from it, and is little short of a mania.

The Press is always reporting that tycoons have taken to the country.

I quote that astute observer of the passing scene Paul Tanfield of the *Daily Mail*:

'Millionaire take-over tycoon, Charles Clore, has quietly taken over motor-car magnate Lord Rootes' 2,000-acre estate, Stype, in Berkshire.

Stype gave its name to Lord Rootes' fine herd of Aberdeen Angus cattle. Mr Clore is starting his own beef herd – he already owns Lord Rootes' magnificent flock of Hampshire Down Sheep.

So now there is confusion at agricultural shows. Does the Stype type refer to Lord Rootes' cattle, moved to new pastures, to Mr Clore's beef, or even to sheep?'

All rich men, it appears, fall for the lure of the farm and the open air. William Hickey, prince of observers of the social scene, writes in the *Daily Express*: 'The Gaekwar of Baroda (51) has bought Monteagle pig farm in the village of Yateley, Hampshire.' And constantly, Mr Hickey, who has a quick eye for the sports and pastimes of the rich, comments on this 'back to the land' movement among the tycoons.

You, Entwistle, think you are immune from the pull of the country, the wind and the rain, the wet grass and the mud, the flowers in spring, and the pink coat of the winter months? You are not. It does not matter whether you come from Salford or Shoreditch, from Harrow or Hull, the country will get you in the end.

It is the secret ambition of all very successful men to become simple country gentlemen. Disraeli, the crafty old fox, knew this when he ordered peacocks to decorate his garden. 'A terrace without peacocks,' he is reported to have said. 'Why, that would be like an empire without an emperor.'

How right he was.

So you, Entwistle, now a Director of Gargantuan Steel, on friendly terms with Sir Walter, and good friends too with the other members of the Board, you will wish to make a move from that comfortable villa of yours, furnished on the H Plan, and take to the country. Why? You have outgrown these surroundings that, a few short years ago, seemed so wonderful to you and your wife.

'I am no snob,' you will rightly claim, 'it just seems that we don't have much in common with our neighbours here any more. In any case I should like the children brought up in good fresh air. . . .'

I understand. It's the great migration. You are going to become the business man who lives in the country but has that convenient flat in London.

And how right you are! Why should you now live in London where, during the winter, the air is so foul that it lays a black excretion on the world every morning? The English countryside is still the loveliest in the world. One has only got to travel to realize this. Once you have endured the hot, barren rocks of Italy, or the endless miles of desolation of the American West, you will come back to the coloured counties of Britain and thank God for so lovely a land.

So it's the great move. But to where? The people to avoid, as if you didn't know, are the estate agents.

They are the most unscrupulous sharks in London. Go and look for yourself. Take out the beige Rover. House-hunt. It's great fun. May I suggest Norfolk, largely undiscovered by British business men, or Sussex, dis-covered, but not yet overcrowded? The Catholic poets knew how good Sussex was:

> 'I will build me a house with deep thatch
>   To shelter me from the cold
> And there shall the Sussex songs be sung
>   And the story of Sussex told.'

You've found a place you both love? Canon Court, near Arundel? But how very clever of you, Entwistle. And Canon Court is the chief house of the little village of Great Thorne Magna (pop. 431)?

The traditional home of the squire? Perfect. Move in.

You really are taking to potential millionairedom like a woman to a new hat.

But may I give you a few hints? You will be sur-rounded now by country people. The fact that you are a Director of Gargantuan Steel will mean nothing to them. They will say, tolerantly, that you are some-thing in the City. Your whole future will be bound up with the classification of Society they place you in. If, clearly, you belong to 'the gentry', a phrase they still use, believe it or not, your path is smooth and clear.

'Don't ride over seeds, keep your temper and never you tell 'em a lie,' roared Kipling in a burst of grand-seigneur fervour. May I add a few tips?

Take it easy, as the grass grows on the weirs. Accept the unhurried measure of the country. Don't worry if the people at the Castle do not dash round the morning after you have moved in to grasp your hand. They know all about you already. They have spies, in the form of agents, bailiffs, and labourers, all over this county – and they have been here a long time. You will be accepted into the county Society – but slowly. The one activity you can take up that will convince one and all that you are acceptable is some form of blood sport. You must kill, Entwistle, and kill quickly.

Can you ride? No? What a pity. At least your children need not suffer from this appalling handicap. And your wife can, as we know, teach them all about horses. This is the quickest, surest cut to the heart of the country. While the little woman turns out – beauti-fully habited – on those frosty winter mornings, the children can follow on ponies.[1] And you can follow in the comfort of the beige Rover, soon to be replaced by a more affluent car.

There is a lot of piffle talked these days about the cruelty of good old English sports. You and I know,

[1] If they are lucky the children can even be 'blooded', a perfectly beastly custom of smearing the child with the dead animal's blood.

Entwistle, that foxes and hares love to be hunted to death and eaten alive by a pack of hounds.

As you, yourself, cannot hunt, you can at least shoot – remember those dates for game destruction I gave you? And you can fish. Fly-fish, of course.

This art and sport has nothing whatever to do with the popular pastime of the cads who catch coarse fish with bait. You, Entwistle, fish for salmon, or trout, or salmon-trout, from March 15th to the end of September. The cads do not fish at this time of year. They pursue their curious hobby in the winter months.

You will, I feel, enjoy fly-fishing, apart from its agreeable social cachet. The equipment is fascinating. The rod – from Hardy – the creel, the reel, the line, the gut, and the minute artificial flies which you can even 'tie' yourself. They have enchanting names like Blue Upright, Devon Rose, Cardew's Killer, and so on. I once taught a millionaire to fly-fish. I was a boy at the time. He was in his sixties. He was a very apt pupil. He had made a million in the wholesale-grocery business. The Herald's College fixed him up with arms and the accoutrements. He bought a village in Devon and commissioned Lutyens to build him a Norman castle. It is the only modern Norman castle in England. The old man was perfect; cunning, honest, humorous, blunt. The sons and nephews are now so important in the West Country that I just dare not mention them.

74

But it shows you, Entwistle, all these country doors are open to the millionaire returning to the land that bred him.

May I add just one word about the children? Two girls and also a boy. Do not slip them into Sherborne. Put the boy down for Eton and the girls for Roedean. It's the best investment you will ever make.[1]

[1] It takes ten years to educate a member of the B.U.C., five years at a preparatory school, and five years at a public school. In addition there may be three years at either Oxford or Cambridge unless the young man is going into the Navy or Army. The total cost, including the university, is around five thousand pounds, but this can be insured against. And the finished product, if reasonably bright, will earn not less than an average of eighty thousand pounds in his lifetime, often, of course, much more. No money investment returns so great and sure a dividend.

7

DIRECTOR STATUS

WELL, Entwistle, what with being a Director of Gargantuan Steel, acquiring Canon Court, moving out of management into the sphere of the executives, the last few years have been exciting enough. You have worked and worked and worked, and now you are beginning to reap.

Mind you to the men at the top, whether in business or in Government, you are still small fry. It is as well that you should remember this. 'Mr Entwistle' may be a name to conjure with in Gargantuan Steel, you may even have been heard of by the steel tycoons of Germany, Japan, and America. But in Britain at the top they hardly know you yet. You are no richer than your rural neighbours who are also City gents disguised as countrymen. You are just a successful City man.

The next step you have to consider is whether this, for you, is the end of the road, or whether you are going to make another great thrust forward to millionairedom. Being you there is no doubt about it. You set your sights early. You will never lower them now.

Now millionairedom may mean that you have, at this stage, to make a big break. Rather like the break that every barrister has to make when he 'takes Silk'[1] and can no longer accept junior briefs. You have reached the top, or nearly the top, in Gargantuan Steel. The Chairmanship still beckons – or does it? Is there a quiet understanding of the powers that be that a member of Sir Walter's family – who hold a majority of shares – should always be Chairman? Is young Play-bright, now young no longer – he has even learned the story of steel – going to slip in before you as he did once before? I think it is highly probable.

The British have an absolute passion for being governed by families they recognize. Even the Labour Party throws up convulsively whenever it is suggested that a member of the working class might become the Party leader.

Find out how the land lies. If the way is really blocked, it is time you made the one great move of your life.

It is time you joined the Board of Chicago Steel who are opening their mammoth English subsidiary in South Wales. A prophet is not without honour . . . Now the Chicago Steel boys may know just how good you

[1] The legal profession rob the unsuspecting layman by a complicated hocus-pocus which divides them into barristers and solicitors, and barristers into 'Juniors' and 'Silks', or Queen's Counsel. This leads to a gratifying duplication of fees all round.

are. They will pay you as little as they can, but it will still be a great deal. It may even be that when Sir Walter has gone, and our Mr Playbright has not been the success expected, Gargantuan will ask you to go back. If that happens your salary and interest and bonus will be astronomical, for no one is more appreciated than the old boy who has made good among the foreigners.

I do not have to tell you that resignation and reappointment are very delicate matters. You must so arrange it that Gargantuan are distraught at losing you, Chicago Steel delighted to get you, and the world at large following the Entwistle fortunes with astonishment and envy.

That curious conglomeration of interests and interlocking finance which we call the City must now take note of your movements. If Gargantuan Steel drop a few points in the stock market as a result of your departure it will not do you any harm. For around you now the mantle of the great man, Entwistle the wizard, is being drawn. You are breaking the barriers in all directions. You have real Director status. You have arrived, though this is far from the end of the road.

Many kinds of straws will show which way the favourable wind is blowing. You may easily be asked to stand for Parliament. In the Tory interest that is. Will you accept? The answer is probably: No. Politics for business men are usually a waste of time. They are the road to honours – not to millionairedom. If you become – when you become – a millionaire, you will be honoured in any case, at least you can be a knight, or, if you really want to found a family, a baronet.

Yet it is flattering to be asked. Should you be offered a safe seat it might be worth considering it. You would meet in the House many of the men who control banking, insurance, and big business. You will be on the fringe of great events and will know all the useful information which the House of Commons sometimes knows before even Fleet Street and the Stock Exchange. If, as you suggested, towards the end, you intend to become a financier as well as a business man, 'the House' is one of the places where certain kinds of information can be obtained. Especially about the steel industry.

If you do accept nomination make sure it is for a seat where the majority is around ten thousand. No anxiety there. You will have a first-rate agent, and a good secretary. Probably two days a month will suffice to 'run' your Constituency.[1] And you will like the House of Commons. True it is as ill-equipped as an English public school – which, in certain respects, it resembles – but the atmosphere is pleasant, especially

[1] Your Constituency party will try to 'run' you. Do not allow this.

for back-benchers. Only at the top are there no friends in the green-eyed jungle of Westminster.

Even if you do not enter the House of Commons I am afraid you cannot get out of rendering public service altogether. It is the tradition. You may well be asked to be a Justice of the Peace. You really should not refuse. It is one of the few completely straightforward

...no friends in the green-eyed jungle of Westminster.

honours left. You get absolutely nothing from it. In Britain we have devised this brilliant means of having all our minor judicial work done free, except for the small number of stipendiary magistrates in great cities.

When you accept you'll have to study Stone's *Justices' Manual*. Beyond that your solicitor-clerk will keep you, and your brother and sister magistrates, on the right lines.

Besides you may well find the work fascinating. For to the Police courts come every kind of case – the great murder trial to establish that there is a 'prima facie' case, the angry wife, the aggrieved husband, the speeding motorist, the drunkard, and the thief. These little courts, so excellently conducted, are part and parcel of the life of England, and it is into the upper strata of that Society that you now, whether you like it or not, are being drawn.

You may have set out, Entwistle, not wishing to get involved in Canon Court, and the County, and the Bench, and even Westminster. You may set yourself for a time against the suggestion that you might do useful work on the County Council – free of course. But in the end you will have to give in. For, by a curious process of attraction and extraction, England does not allow her sons to become millionaires without giving service. Some types of service you may avoid by a modern form of scutage – the handsome donation – but all you cannot shirk.

And I am happy it is so, for during the last twenty years you have had your eyes fixed far too firmly on the glittering prize of great wealth. Now you are being gently diverted, and disgorged.

If, as I suggested, Gargantuan Steel might now welcome you back as Chairman, go back. You can make your own terms. You are worth a quarter of a million now. That is much more than a quarter of the way to your goal. How do you make it a round million? Let me introduce you to the City and the Stock Market.

. . . there is an alchemy that can double your horde . . .

8

THE HIGHER SKULDUGGERY

YOUR problem now, Entwistle, is comparatively simple. You wish to convert your quarter of a million pounds into a million, and thus achieve the target you have been aiming at from those very early and almost forgotten days when you first came from Lancashire to London.

Happily there is an alchemy that can double your horde and more without you having to do any additional work. Or at least you will only be called upon to do work that has now become second nature to you.

So far you have been a business man. Your story has been part of the fine, rugged story of British Steel. Your present wealth has come from those furnaces – and from your brains, and industry, and integrity.

Now you can become a financier and wax really rich.

You must tread a little gently at first, for you are now entering the most powerful secret society on earth, the City of London. At the apex of this the wealthiest square miles in the worlds are the Bank of England, the big five Banks, the great commercial Banks, the

Stock Exchange, the great Insurance Companies and those thousands of private-enterprise British firms whose activities span the world – the bridge builders, the utility stores, the Gold and Tin Companies, the Property Companies, and the Hire Purchase Finance Companies. The last two have only just joined the hierarchy.

Until recently they were suspect, but the City has one rule which it always obeys even in the face of social prejudice: 'If there is money in it we must move in.'

The most amusing example of the working of this rule was the recent 'take-over' by the Banks of the Hire Purchase firms. For years the Hire Purchase corporations had been beyond the pale. The City attitude was – for the general public not for themselves: 'If you can't pay for it don't buy.' It was a curious attitude coming from an establishment built up on the credit principle. Probably the real reason why the City detested the Hire Purchase people was that they were considered to be upstarts and dubious upstarts at that. But then Hire Purchase prospered – outrageously. The City and the City Banks did a volte face overnight. Where before there had been frowns now there were sunny, extrovert smiles. . . .

Hire Purchase was taken into the fold. I tell you this, Entwistle, to remind you that to win friends, gain prestige, and make money as a financier, it is not your ability that matters so much as whether you know the right people, the people at the top. All these people, or nearly all, went to the same schools. For instance:

I am looking down the list of the Governor and Court of the Bank of England and the Board of a national – and international – Insurance Company, which tells me where the Directors learned their first lessons.

'Eton and King's College, Cambridge.'
'Marlborough and Corpus Christi, Cambridge.'
'Eton and Sandhurst.'
'Eton and Magdalen College, Oxford.'
'Eton and Trinity College, Cambridge.'
'Harrow and St John's, Cambridge.'

One Director appears to have been educated at a Council school. Well, well, the people will creep in anywhere if you give them half a chance. They come out of the woodwork, I expect.

So you see, Entwistle, you are at a disadvantage. But it is a disadvantage that, by the wise fashioning of your affairs during the last few years, you have largely overcome. You have overcome it by joining the Junior Conservative (where the P.M. drops in on a Sunday morning for a dry sherry). You have over-

come it by becoming the lord and master of Canon
Court and the squire of your charming little Sussex
village. You have dispelled it by marrying your tall,
aquiline, horsy wife who neighs in the nicest way at
your equally sporting friends and neighbours. And of
course your children, young Alasdair and Elizabeth,
and little Nicolette, are so horsy and blue and upper
crust that no one for a moment would imagine that
father had started so very recently in Paradise Street
in Salford.

This is all greatly to your credit. You are not a
hypocrite. You have just played the game according to
the rules – and won, which is much better than being
ordered off the field because you insist that you do not
like the rules of the game.

Now I mentioned, much earlier, that British business,
and this includes the City, has one redeeming quality
that ensures its survival, indeed its virility and longevity.
It never keeps a man out if he is good enough – and
you are good enough. So you may come in. You may
join the Board of a number of national concerns.

For last year you became Sir John. One day you
opened your *Times*, glanced at the Birthday Honours,
and under the K.B.E.s there it was:

'John Hardcastle Entwistle, for social and political
services.'

The only man who has seen it before you is your

'Will you be needing
the car, Sir John?'

man, Paget, the only manservant except old William the gardener that you keep – in these democratic days – at Canon Court.

For Paget this is a proud moment. He is thrilled and delighted. He makes a quite unnecessary tour of the house to find you and your wife. He finds you in your study smiling at *The Times*. He knocks, smiles, and says: 'Will you be needing the car, Sir John?'

Then he finds your wife pruning roses and says: 'Will there be any guests for the weekend, m'lady?'

It was almost worth getting this honour for Paget. And for yourself, too. When you kneel before this regal smiling young woman and she touches your shoulder with a sword and says: 'Arise, Sir John,' you know that you are now in the procession, the grand procession of Britain, with its velvet and purple tradition rooted in history.[1]

How many Companies should you become a Director of? I suggest not more than a dozen. And most of them should be Directorships of firms whose business you understand, steel and its many allied trades. But you should try for at least one Bank.

It is a long time ago that Banks were private and the owner asked you into his parlour for sherry and cake while you discussed the financing of that shipment of

[1] Honours are no longer sold in Britain as they were in good Mr Lloyd George's golden days. But they are the object of one of the mystical wangles so dear to British hearts.

spices from the Indies. But the tradition, and immense prestige, of the British Banks go on. To this day they are the finest, and in some respects the most efficient, Banks in the world. Yet they have never lost their profound conviction that it is the man who matters.

The Banks, still run in this personal way, are very much tied up with the Treasury and the Chancellor who, of course, is in cahoots with the Prime Minister. So the Banks, for you, are prestige-plus.

You have two types to choose from. One of the big five. They are the very top of the banking tree. And the lesser known Commercial Bankers, people like Lazards. They finance the financiers, and industry in general. When you are asked to join the Board of a Bank such as this you have achieved one of your major victories. You have arrived.

Financially this 'City', of which you are now becoming a key figure, is still the greatest in the world. Its ramifications are greater than New York or Zurich.

A very large number of American Insurance Companies themselves insure against loss with Lloyds of London. The tendrils of City finance are world-wide. It is a majestic empire you are entering.

The City has persuaded itself – it is cardinal doctrine – that what is good for the City is good for Britain, good for the British Empire, good for the British Commonwealth, good for that vast stretch of financial pact and influence the sterling area, and so, in the end, good for the world.

That convenient, and not altogether fallacious, faith makes the City practically the right hand of God in matters of finance.

Only very recently have cracks appeared in the shining armour of the City's infallibility. The Bank Rate Tribunal of 1957 was the first major tremor of disbelief, and, although the heretics were routed, the British public heard a Director of the Bank of England contemplate the switch of money from Britain to North America, during a sterling crisis, in these never-to-be-forgotten words:

'Again this is anti-British and harmful to sterling, but, on balance, if one is free to do so, it makes sense to me.'

One does not wish to prolong the agony of that appalling evidence. For the first time the British public thought they saw a vision they did not like. A vision of a City so money-mad that even financial treason would be justified – a City more concerned with its own wealth than the country's good. The truth, you will find, Entwistle, falls somewhere between the two pictures. The City is not altruistic, not essentially patriotic, but it is convinced that by the mighty striving of free enterprise, free money, and the rendering of valuable services throughout the world, it is doing itself good – which is certain – and doing the country good, too.

Well, your Directorships will come in very handy. Your income will shoot up from around six thousand a year to around thirty thousand a year. Unfortunately your net income, after deducting tax, will increase very little. And your total wealth hardly at all. So let me introduce you to the Share Market where your gains – thank God and the Tories – are not taxed at all, except for a trifling stamp duty. Here you can make your new wealth on information you gain through your new connexions and friends. Finally I will tell you how to keep more of this money from the diabolical tax people. Canon Court will have to be enlarged. You must buy that two thousand acres that the Beauclerk family wish to sell. It's back to the land for you, Entwistle.

It's enormous fun this last great move. The expense account comes into it, too. It's brigandage, but it's legal, and, at the end, you'll be home, high and dry, with your million.

... hear all the city news at the
earliest possible moment ...

9

THE MARKET

You are now in a position, Sir John, to hear all the City news at the earliest possible moment. It can be very valuable to you. Addison said that 'Despatch is the essence of business' and he was right. Information may mean a fortune for you if acted on at the right time, which is usually immediately, before the others have woken up, or got round to it.

You will need a reliable, loyal, and alert broker. Loyal is probably the operative adjective. There are times when the jobbers who deal in specific categories of shares have persuaded brokers or their clients to buy shares that show ominous trends. If your broker is not loyal to you there is a temptation to 'unload' these hot potatoes on to you. It will be done in the nicest possible way of course, the quiet, dignified, British way, but the result will be much the same – as if you had been stabbed in the back.

The market, alone, should provide you with the means of making up your fortune to the million mark at the present time.

As long as we have peace, plus astronomical nuclear and space spending, the market will continue to boom, periodically. Little restraint will be placed on the City, or on the Banks, or on the Hire Purchase Companies, or on the Stock Exchange. The really clever investor will have ideal conditions to operate in.

And best of all, the Labour Party, once a real bogey, now intends to do nothing drastic about it, even if they ever get back to power. All the Socialist fervour and faith of fifty years has been washed overboard by Gentleman Gaitskell, the skipper who has degutted the Labour Party of Socialism, so that it is now a damp squib which the public, rightly, reject.[1]

This is perfect for you, Sir John. And the temper and climate of the day favour you. Materialism is almost universally accepted. When the public see worldly old men bossing the Church of England they say to themselves: 'Let's make ourselves comfortable here on earth, even if we can't get a salary of £15,000 a year.' This is just what you want. It leads to a boom in commodities such as the world has never seen before.

The West, the virile, thrusting, free-enterprise West, does not want war or peace. It wants things just as they are, with great economies boosted by vast 'defence' expenditure. If peace came tomorrow, there would be

[1] I wrote these words before the 'Sack Gaitskell' movement really got under way in the Labour Party.

so much wailing on Wall Street that the tears would flood New York. That is why the Russian peace offers get such a cold reception. The fear that it might be genuine. . . .

So go ahead, Sir John, in this booming economy. It won't worry you – unduly – that the old-age pensioners are, just, not starving. You get rich – quick, while the going is good.

As I have suggested it will probably be possible for you to reach your goal without stepping too deeply into the swift-flowing currents of the City. You will not have to promote Companies. If you ever do take care that they are very successful promotions. In the City nothing succeeds anything like success. You must be six times over subscribed by noon on the day you make your shares available to the public. In this way the legend of Sir John Entwistle will ride on.

Remember the City, and the Stock Exchange in particular, is as jumpy as a nervous cat about world news. If, for instance, tomorrow President Eisenhower had a slight stroke, the world markets would suffer a temporary but perceptible set-back. If there is an assassination in Rabat or Baghdad oil shares will dive. If the Prime Minister here makes a depressing speech, shares will waver. If he is confident, buoyant, scanning the horizon eagerly with that sly smile of his, even dithering shares assume a rock-like quality, and good shares zoom.

Mind you, Sir John, you may get one or two slaps. Once upon a time, when there was a depression in Lancashire, an astute and able London financier decided that the time was ripe to 'take over' some of the Lancashire mills, and resell them. He made a fortune. But the people of Lancashire suffered. When the astute financier suggested a visit to Manchester the answer was:

'I wouldn't go there, Sir William. Your name fair stinks in Lancashire.' Disconcerting.

And when the same good citizen sent a cheque for twenty-five pounds (jolly generous) to aid the poor of Burnley in a cold winter he got his cheque back from the Mayor with a very rude endorsement.

Which brings me to the take-over bid. This is a technique that you should not have to adopt, but that you should know all about.

The first step is to look round for some great solid conservative business whose Directors, for purposes of their own, and because it is second nature to them, have been secreting the Company's wealth in a variety of ways.

Let us call the firm Bruce's. Now Bruce's superfine Scottish whisky ('A dram for delight') is an old family business.

The Bruce family have been diligently distilling and blending fine whisky for generations. For years it was a nice quiet business, prosperous; yes, but not ostentatiously so. Then the Americans discovered real whisky and compared it with the muck they had been drinking for years. The demand for Bruce's for export became fabulous.

The extrovert Yankee reaction to this would have been: 'Oh, boy, Bruce's is bigger and better than ever!'

But the Bruce-family reaction was: 'Still a family

and personal firm, not a drop sold until it's fifteen years old. We are managing nicely.'

And the Bruce ordinary shares in the market stay steady at twenty-six shillings. Then comes our take-over gentleman. He sends his spies to discover the real worth of the Bruce set-up. He finds that the real value of the shares cannot be less than two pounds. So he starts to buy, quietly, under a number of names, a little here, a lot there. And he is going, bless him, to make a double profit. He is buying an undervalued commodity in the first place, and, in the second place, the buying, with a growing momentum, will stimulate interest in Bruce's shares. The public, through their brokers, will all want to be in on this. They will buy Bruce's like mad.

At the right moment, when the buying craze has reached its zenith, or just before, he will let the public have back the shares which they are now crying for at three pounds which, as we know, is more than Bruce's are worth. Or, alternatively, he will march on, himself, and clinch the matter by obtaining control of Bruce's, at under two pounds a share, before the Bruce family have rallied. If he does take over he may stream-line the old firm, boost its profits, do away with all this 'fifteen years to mature' nonsense. Either way he wins to the tune of many thousands of pounds. He may well make a fortune in one swoop, one devastating raid on the smug, complacent concerns of Britain who are not really prepared to cope with the take-over character.

Above all, Sir John, you will have to keep your ear to the ground and your nose on the trail. There are men who can smell money. It has, to them, a sweet aroma, as unmistakable as the sickly sweetness of opium. They follow the scent as relentlessly, and with much the same bloodcurdling feeling of satisfaction, as your hound its stag.

Soon they know the kill must come and they can dig their long fangs into more and more money, a sublime and joyous chase.

The opportunities that present themselves to you will be innumerable and constant. Picking out the best, the surest, and the most lucrative will evoke your money flair.

You will be able to adopt the brilliant technique of Mr Charles Clore. A Company owning say a hundred shops comes to your notice. The chances are they stand in the balance sheets at pre-war values. Buy control of the Company, sell the shops (or most of them) to Insurance Companies as investment – and rent them back. That way you get the business and you get most of your money back, either to repay loans used to buy the business, or to finance new take-overs.

This method of business, entirely straightforward, can have brilliant results.

Keep a watchful eye on the old-fashioned business that has been 'in the family' for years, possibly for a century. It is quite likely that the Directors have been content with a profit-taking level that would have caused a riot if there had been outside shareholders. You will be able to explain to the family owners how heavily death duties bear on privately owned Companies, and, with luck, persuade them to sell a controlling interest.

Then the big break. Complete modernization. Doubling of profits within a comparatively short space of time. Then the sale of shares to the public, eager to buy – 'Lists closed 10·01 owing to heavy over-subscription.' A ballot for shares, the sign of success. You, Sir John, retain a goodly block yourself. The jobbers will be round imploring you to part with these to keep the market going. Good business for you, Sir John.

As funds accumulate you will be able to turn your attention in other directions. Your eye roams over the possibilities. Cannot you muscle in on one of the syndicates that sponsor Commercial TV? A tycoon has described TV as a licence to print money. A charmingly graphic phrase.

There are advantages in hiring out TV sets rather than selling them. Look into this. And the do-it-yourself boom, this may provide you with a profitable sideline.

Money attracts money. You have become a magnet, Sir John, to draw the gold towards you. By your industry, integrity, and extreme astuteness you have made your million. You have followed the rules that I have put forward, and elaborated, and explained. Let me recapitulate.

You have become a magnet

1. Never waver. Be absolutely determined always. Never lower your sights.

2. Work, and work, and work.

3. Marry a horsy wife and gradually insinuate yourself into British upper-crust society.

4. Have absolute faith. Believe that money brings you all you desire.

5. Wrap around yourself, as you rise, the mantle of greatness.

6. Never cheat, but do not be soft. It is a hard world. Be harder. But, and this is the test, at the same time, obviously, a good fellow.

Nothing can stop you. Nothing has stopped you. You have honours, great wealth, a weary but faithful wife, and fashionable children. You've played the game according to the rules, and you've won.

Even now there is one other matter I must tell you all about before I leave you. Are you going to accept an income of under ten thousand a year and let the tax people take twenty? Don't be silly. Get out the expense-accounts book, and let us consider that additional two thousand acres of England you have recently added to the manor of Canon Court.

IO

DOWN ON THE FARM

Your income, now, Sir John, has reached mammoth proportions. But your income tax and surtax are even more fantastic. It is up to you to reduce drastically this vast flow of money to the tax gatherers. To accomplish this you need a firm of smart – but entirely reputable – tax accountants. How about Simpson, Battle, and Blarney? They are very good people, up to all the tricks of the trade. Chancellors come and go but Simpson, Battle, and Blarney go on for ever.

Your brief for Simpson, Battle, and Blarney, Sir John, is simple: How do I pay as little as possible? But you will, with the discretion that you have learnt over the years, phrase it differently. 'I shall be obliged if you will review these figures and see what tax economies can be effected.' Something like that. As if you didn't know.

Simpson, Battle, and Blarney will tell you, Sir John, that the best way for you to get more value for your money is to farm. And that is very fortunate, for already you have Canon Court and the land that goes with it, wonderful pasture down by the river, good grain land up to the church, as well as coverts to harbour your pheasants and foxes for the Ditchling Hunt.

The essential principles for farmers such as yourself, Sir John, are simple, though their application may become more complicated every year.

The first principle is that you should be a *real* farmer, with real bulls, real corn, and real mud, but, at the same time, a farmer whose accounts show a regular, substantial, and indisputable annual loss.

The second principle is an extension of the first. Now that you are what the tax people describe, with their happy Latin flair, as a bona-fide farmer, you and your wife and children, relatives and guests, your dogs and your servants, can all live on the farm, and live very well indeed, free; that is to say all the horses you ride, the wagons and shooting-brakes you run, all the milk and honey, partridges and ducks, chickens and lamb, and vegetables you eat, even your home-made cider,[1] will all go down on the farm account as living expenses.

Naturally you must play your part. You must look like a farmer, at least at weekends. Nothing gives a City

[1] All you need to make home-brew beer and cider is a whitewashed shed, the vats, the apples, the malt, and a good book of instructions. The beer can be made to have at least twelve per cent alcoholic content—a gentleman's beer.

The making of your own cider and the brewing of your own beer is a sine qua non for potential country gentlemen, both in Britain and in the Southern States of America. It's great fun. You must try it.

gent that genuine earthy look as convincingly as Harris
tweed and gaiters. Take a trudge over your pastures
thus attired. You have the odour and aura of England.
You are genuine.

*Accept the unhurried measure
of the country*

And then, Sir John, you must master the jargon.

Words like rotation of crops, heifers (a young cow
that has not yet calved), silage, 'ditchin' and hedgin',
should come naturally to you. And it would be a very
great help if you could talk farming with the real
farmers – who are trying to make their farms pay – who
are your neighbours. Thus:

107

'What do 'e reckon turnips will fetch next year, Sir John?'

'Difficult to say, Willum. Maybe five pun a ton, maybe more. . . .'

And as you stand there, Sir John, from Friday to Sunday night, in your Harris tweeds, well gaitered, the Sussex mud clogging your boots, pulling on your briar pipe, who could doubt that here is one of the island breed, the men who have brought in the food – and were sometimes exempted from military service – in two world wars, the men of Britain who are, we say, the best farmers in the world?

I must tell you now that there is a real danger lurking in the farming-loss racket. It is perfectly sound so long as you are ruthless, determined to show a loss. You will have an agent and each year, as the accounts are due to be cast, you will run over the figures with him. If there is any danger of a profit you must put your foot down.

'We must build a road through the spinney, Bolting.'

'A road, Sir John? What for?'

'When the men are working at Little Plover they have to walk through the spinney or round by the old bakery. It's not right. This farm is the last word in efficiency. Communications must be in keeping with our code.'

'Very well, Sir John, but it will be expensive. . . .'

'How expensive?'

Here Mr Bolting makes a few hasty calculations.

'Can't come to less than two thousand pounds, Sir John.'

'Two thousand puns, eh? Excellent. Put the work in hand straight away and see the debit goes into this account.'[1]

Now that danger I spoke of may develop when you have been farming at Canon Court some years. You get tired of hearing your farmer friends whisper to you that they cleared a nice little profit on the barley. . . . And Mr Bolting may have made the farm so efficient – sorry, put the land into such good heart – that it is becoming almost impossible to show a loss on Canon Court.

Farming is booming in a quiet, secretive kind of way. The fact that no farmer admits this really is not the point. Ask them of course and they always give the same reply:

'Terrible, zur, terrible. Worst I've known in ten years.'

But look at their farms and their standard of living

---

[1] I have already stressed the necessity of thinking rich. Your potential millionaire starts this very early. Later he develops curious but characteristic money habits. Only last month a London dentist was surprised to receive back a bill he had sent to a tycoon, endorsed with the simple epitaph : 'This is too much.' Only your millionaire can afford to adopt this tone – and these tactics.

and compare it with twenty years ago. There is the
Ford Zodiac parked in the drive. There is the combined
harvester put away in dust sheets in the barn. The only
thing wrong with most British farms is that they are
too small. It may just be possible to show a profit
on a smallholding worked by a family without a wage
bill. But the farms of between eighty and five hundred
acres are uneconomic – unless run on a communal
basis with other small units. Perish the thought.

You, Sir John, do not suffer from this basic handicap.
The two thousand acres you farm is an economic unit.
You can afford to run it with a manager – Mr Bolting,

Canon Court
Farm
Income
═══ 10,000
Expenses
═══ 8,000
Profit £2,000

"We can't show a loss
this year Sir John."

your agent – and workers, very skilled workers, cow-
men, shepherds, grooms, labourers who will only demand, bless their little feudal hearts, an unskilled
wage.

So you may well be up against it. There may come
an account-reviewing day when Mr Bolting will say:

'We can't show a loss this year, Sir John. We really
can't. Look at the figures.'

You look at them and realize you are defeated. At
the same time an awful sensation of pride may seize you.
Canon Court paying! 'One of the most efficient and
successful mixed farms in Britain.' The Friesian herd
famous throughout the world. A model of planned
farming economy. You're lost, Sir John. The country
has got you at last.

From now on you will throw that ghastly phrase
'gentleman farmer' into the sewer. You are a farmer,
now. And standing there in one of your fields by the
river which you have stocked with eight-inch rainbow
trout – from your own hatchery – gazing with pride at
your superb herd of milking cows, their udders a provo-
cative promise of more and more good milk to come,
you know, in your heart, that the witchery of the
English countryside has stolen you away from the
City, that you are a countryman now. You glance at
the sky in instinctive assessment of the weather. . . .

I do not conceal the fact, Sir John, that I am glad it

has worked out this way. I like you better now that you have gone back to your roots, for your grandfather – remember? – was a farm labourer in the old days before his son went to work in Salford, where you were born. Yes, a farm labourer earning twenty-two shillings a week, with a wife and five children. Not in the middle ages. Quite recently, here, in Britain.

Now that you have given up the uneven struggle to make a loss on Canon Court, you really must pay more attention to your business and general-expense accounts. Simpson, Battle, and Blarney will think of all kinds of ways of boosting these 'expenses' of yours and setting them off against tax. But the real move is with you.

The British tax man is upright, diligent, fair, but, luckily for you, Sir John, he is a snob. He will accept that in your position, leading the kind of life you do, a very high standard of expenses is essential, say £10,000 to £15,000 a year. But you must make this outrageous assessment appear possible, even real.

Your yacht, the *Patricia*, must be tracked by William Hickey in his sparkling column:

'And who should turn up but the Entwistles, Sir John bronzed and gay, Lady Entwistle as *soignée* as ever. In the casino later I watched Sir John lose five hundred pounds without batting an eyelid. "Not my day, Hickey," he said. "Never win unless we have a waxing moon. . . ." '

Once a year you and your wife should take the cure at a German spa. Cheltenham, Bath, and Buxton may be better, but for you it's Germany. You just can't afford to be seen wrapped in a king-size bath-towel in Britain.

The only place you can frequent for ten days every year for your health, is that amusingly expensive slimming mansion in Surrey. You will meet all your friends there. Diet: three oranges a day. Price ten guineas a day for one of those lovely front rooms overlooking the park.[1]

If you build up this kind of reputation your expense figures will go through without comment. When they pass through the tax office each year, the Head, Mr Peake, will say: 'Let me have Sir John Entwistle's figures, will you. I always deal with them myself.' Mr Peake takes an odd pride in putting through your outrageous figures. It brings a little warmth and glamour into his own drab life. He almost feels he knows you.

---

[1] Quite recently the super-slimming business, the business of decarbonizing the wealthy, has mushroomed. If, for fifty weeks in the year, you eat too much smoked trout and scampi and jugged hare, drink too much Tio Pepe and white burgundy, it is necessary for you to rest your digestive organs for at least two weeks to avoid obesity and hypertension. A better way of doing this is not to over-indulge, but I am being practical.

...You and your wife should take the cure at a German spa

You have now made your million, John Entwistle. I have told you how to keep it and increase it. Yours has been quite a life, hasn't it? Better than the storybooks. Your dreams come true. But before we draw the curtain let me give you some very concrete hints on income preservation.

II

THE FRATERNITY

Now, Sir John, that you have made your million it is right and proper that you should know something of your fellow millionaires, for there is a fraternity among millionaires that does not exist among men who are merely rich.

The fraternity has, like Britain, no written Constitution, and it may be said not to exist – officially. This has the advantage of making its unwritten rules very pliable, its code easily changeable, and the admission of new members a discreet, unadvertised acceptance.

Do you doubt that there is a freemasonry among millionaires? Watch the millionaires themselves and you will be convinced. Mr Macmillan (is he a millionaire? Probably) will drop in at a cocktail party given by Mr Harold Samuel. What have they in common? Yes, you're right. If you are very, very rich, Dukes will talk to you when you meet them at a point to point – 'Hulloa, Entwistle. Lovely day, what? Know anything for the next race?' They will even allow their wives to sit on committees with your wife. Yes, there is a fraternity – and a sorority as well.

The millionaires of Britain are the most complicated in the world. American millionaires are delightfully simple in contrast. They are divided into the *ancien riche*, those who accumulated before 1900, and the *nouveau riche*, the twentieth-century sharks. Soviet millionaires, such as Mr Khrushchev, are also uncomplicated. Soviet millionaires do not handle money. They just take it in roubles, and gold plate, and motor-cars, and travelling vouchers, but they are as far removed from the common herd as you British millionaires. They just don't have that bulging bank account. They do not need it.

Millionairedom in Britain is entirely open and respectable. It does not have to stoop to subterfuge and camouflage. For it starts at the top, with the House of Windsor.

No one knows, exactly, how much good solid gold good solid Queen Victoria left, but it was a mint. The old lady was naturally frugal and she reigned decade after decade, increasing her stupendous fortune. Every now and then an Indian potentate would give her a gem worth a Queen's ransom for good measure.

Good, guttural King (baccarat and girls) Edward VII tried his very best, in his halcyon days as King, to reduce the old lady's fortune, but with very little success. He died before he could really tackle the job.

The vast wealth of the House of Windsor has never been in danger since. Dear old King George V, the sailor King, was gruffly economical. The Duke of Windsor was, well, careful. King George VI did what he thought was right, and extravagance was not in his code; while Madam, our present Monarch, seems to show all those admirably careful and acquisitive traits that enabled Queen Victoria to start this great golden ball rolling.[1]

With this royal background, millionairedom in Britain is here to stay. The only real threat to the British millionaires was Clause 4 of the Labour Party Constitution, which pledged that party to a Socialist State, but now Mr Gaitskell has extended, amplified, elongated, and explained Clause 4. It no longer counts for a row of beans. Winchester has thrown the Socialist State out of the window. The millionaires are safe.

And what a grand and glorious band they are!

First, after the Monarch, in this glittering procession, come the ducal millionaires, those resplendent old-timers, the Dukes of Westminster, Norfolk, and Devonshire. And what examples they give us of the fraternity

---

[1] It has been pointed out that Prince Philip is not infected with the saving virus, being a typical Balkan Prince, and lavish. Well, damn it, somebody must spend the money. A jolly Norwegian was heard to remark in Oslo recently that the British Navy might not be what it was, but that the royal yacht was smashing.

and sorority. For at Coronations you will always see an Earl Marshal – a Duke of Norfolk of course – stage-managing the unforgettable show, while a Duchess of Devonshire is often a Mistress of the Robes. What are her duties? I refuse to tell you.

There are a few non-Dukes in the same class: the Earls of Derby for instance who own large slices of Lancashire. But the Dukes waxed rich on owning London. They were, and are, Lords of the West End. Go to the office of Grosvenor Estates in Davies Street. In the magnificent panelled waiting-room you may still see the red-and-gold, and crowned, sedan-chair, complete with strawberry leaves, in which their Graces of Westminster were carried through London.

Next, Sir John, come the old industrial millionaires. People like the Chamberlains, the Wedgwoods, and the Baldwins. Early-nineteenth-century business men who grew with Britain and her Empire. So great was their probity, and their pride, that they did not seek honours. They were content to be millionaires, and good employers.

The great newspapers account for a unique category, for the Harmsworths, and the Kemsleys, the Express group, and its rivals, gave birth to an oligarchy of brains and wealth, of which Lord Beaverbrook is still the active doyen. Useful people to know these, Sir John. Their City editors, too.

In the world of finance there is still a line drawn between the old banking families and the new financiers, but the line is fast vanishing. Fings may not be what they used ter be, but they are what they are, and we must march with the times.

Hire Purchase has become respectable. Property is no longer frowned on. Television is now the darling of the Banks. For the door to millionaire mansions is always locked, but can always be opened by discreet gentlemen with the right golden key.

And, finally, of course, we have the boy from the back-streets who has made good. Of this vintage are you, Sir John, and it is, perhaps, the most honourable group of all.

Very few professional men ever become millionaires. They may well become famous. They may build their own fortunes – 'Smith of my own fortune' proudly declared the first Lord Birkenhead in his motto; but these men are not for us to consider for their aim has been fame, not money.

Foreign millionaires have a bouquet all their own. Mr Onassis has become a legend, and Sir Winston Churchill must know his way around the Onassis yacht almost as well as his weather-beaten Greek host. The world and arrows of outrageous fortune can hardly touch you if you own enough tankers. Even the greatest figures will come and make history on your ship.

So the pattern of the millionaires is the rich, varied pattern that England favours in her social fabric. The vigour and variety of the British social and industrial scene is reflected in these superbly rich men. The millionaires have nothing in common except their vast wealth.

You will find, Sir John, that being able to write a cheque for any amount at any time solves most of life's difficulties, except the eternal problems of health and happiness. It is an alarming thought that the heart, the liver, the kidneys, and the intestines are no respecters of money. However rich you are a little tumour or a malignant growth can destroy you, and there is nothing very much, beyond employing the best doctors, that you can do about it. However you can help greatly in avoiding illness by not pursuing Mammon so relentlessly after you have achieved your goal. It may well be that the pressure and habits of a lifetime are hard to break. But gently, easily, Sir John, now in your fifties, you should slow down, for it would be nice if you lived on to a ripe old age, a mellow, experienced man with a growing family and many friends.

You will find your fellow millionaires full of tips on longevity. They are as cunning as monkeys, and they have all the diets at their finger-tips. But perhaps a very good general practitioner is the best man to put you on the right lines.

Are millionaires ever happy? They are just as happy and as unhappy as other men. The elusive smiling sprite plays its game with all men and cares not whether they are rich or poor.

Your own good sense, Sir John, that has stood you in such good stead all these years, will have told you that happiness depends largely on your wife and your health. So you will look after both. Your marriage long ago survived the first stormy years and the deeper loyalties

...fellow millionaires full of tips on longevity.

have begun to emerge. This alone will bring you great satisfaction.

If, as a final ambition, you wish to free your spirit from deceit, do not take too seriously the flowers that the world scatters in the paths of the very rich. It is a disconcerting thought that, if you lost your money, these gestures of delight would vanish.

The fraternity may have some difficulty with the needle's eye, but, here on earth, everyone, from Heads of State to head waiters, is moved by the personification of Money.

The world smiles on you now, Sir John. It's the gold dust in their eyes.

12

THEY HAVE THEIR LITTLE WAYS

EVEN these days very few men become millionaires overnight. Certainly you, Sir John, have come up the hard, and gradual way. You have had time to adapt yourself to millionairedom. Now, I must say, Lord of Canon Court, it fits you like a glove. I saw you the other day at Cowdray watching the polo with your wife, your Bentley, a son and daughter-in-law, your shooting-sticks, your expensive luncheon-baskets, and your aura of quiet, composed millionairedom.

You have had time to assume the foibles that even the nicest millionaires are apt to become victims of.

For instance, I rang you up some ten days back. This is what happened.

'May I speak to Sir John, please?'

'Sir John is not available at the moment. Can I help you?'

'Yes. If you would be good enough to get Sir John on the phone for me . . .'

'I'm sorry, Sir John is not here. May I have your name? We could ring you back. . . .'

I gave in. I realized that this indestructible creature was merely guarding the Entwistle fortune as she is paid to do. It is unseemly that millionaires should be attacked by telephone out of the blue like ordinary men.

When you, Sir John, knew who was calling you, you would come through to me. But could I employ these waiting tactics with you? Perish the thought. The Guardian Angel's job would then be to make sure that I was waiting to receive you, receiver in hand.

Strange things happen, however, when millionaires wish to speak to millionaires.

These are difficulties of protocol, as when Emperors meet. Each millionaire has its no-woman entrenched at the telephone. Neither millionaire must be kept waiting. A simultaneous contact must be effected. It is a matter of split-second timing.

I notice, Sir John, that you do not now carry money around with you, at least not when you are in London. In this respect millionaires resemble royalty – with whom they have much in common. As you have found out, all London restaurants and hotels of the first order recognize millionaires like yourself instantly, and are happy to make a discreet note of the bill. A rich man who pays in cash at the Savoy grill at luncheon causes something of a stir. The waiter whispers to the head waiter. Together they carry the unfamiliar notes to the cashier. The customer is an eccentric, obviously.

..millionaires can afford to be eccentric..

The truth is that millionaires can afford to be eccentric, and often are. There is nothing to prevent you, Sir John, adopting your own little badge of oddity. You may insist on the port being passed clockwise, you may wear stocks instead of ties, you may have your shoes laced at the sides or at the back, you need not appear in the telephone book at all, you can daily wear a cabbage rose, hot-house grown, you can do anything you like in the field of eccentricity and the kindly public will forgive you. 'After all,' they will say 'he can afford it.'

What is it, Sir John, that binds millionaires together? I think social delicacy comes into it. They do not feel entirely comfortable with men to whom expense is still a consideration.

When a holiday at Brighton, Cannes, or Hong Kong is equally available to you, it may embarrass you to know that your friend cannot afford a holiday this year. It may even lead to your standing him one, which, on principle, is demoralizing. It is, on the whole, more comfortable to be with men entirely liberated from the shackles that money imposes – men of your own kind.

But far sterner links than these bind the millionaires together. Millionaires know how difficult it is to make the first clever steps that lead to millionairedom. They know that money can accumulate – and evaporate.

They know that they are the objects of envy. They know that millionaires are fair game. Together they feel the strength of unity. Alone, or with others, they fear that they may wander unarmed into enemy territory.

However, as you have found out, Sir John, there are a legion of parasites who are prepared to protect a millionaire from the cold, cruel world.

There are the lawyers, bless their cold, little hearts. They fight by shuffling papers, your papers and other people's papers, so that you, Sir John, may always come out on top. A really good firm of lawyers, dedicated to doing down your opponents, are powerful allies. There is no trick – within the law – that they will not stoop to. You pay them. They are your henchmen. Your interest is their interest. They have no humanity, no morals. You can do, in their name, things that you could not conceivably do yourself.

And then, of course, there are your invaluable accountants. They again are devoted to your interest. They act as a great, comfortable buffer between you and the tax men. They collect your income and pay it into your Bank accounts. Yes, you now have a number of accounts numbered one, two, three, and four, for different purposes. Hand in hand with your accountants are your good friends the Bank.

The Bank love you, Sir John. There is really no other

word for it. You are their ideal, the successful free-enterprise tycoon. Remember that if you should at any time wish to borrow money from them, it should be a good round sum, say a hundred thousand pounds. Never ask for a few thousands. This immediately makes the Bank suspicious. Poor Whittaker Wright was trapped because he asked for too small a loan.

Are people like yourself, Sir John, always going to be with us? Are the millionaires here to stay? I am sure they are.

Long after democracy has seeped into the United States, and plutocracy has come into the open in the Soviet Union, the millionaires of Britain will be going their own way, rich and happy. For, on the whole, they are a discreet, genial body of men. They do not infuriate the populace by vulgar displays of ostentation and extravagance. They build high walls to preserve their privacy. If they are profligate the world does not see it. In public they assume a convincing camaraderie. They might almost be one of us.

A hundred little points arise, as you know, Sir John, while we are protecting you and your money. Your children, for instance, can be profitably kidnapped. This is a revolting crime that does not trouble the likes of us, but can be a nightmare to the likes of you. It is as well to screen your servants very carefully. Then your signature, Sir John. Such a valuable signature! Remember what happened when a clerk called Goudie found he could reproduce the signature of Mr Hudson, the Soap King. One hundred and sixty thousand pounds stolen in nine months. Of course the Bank of Liverpool had to pay, not Mr Hudson, but still it was sacrilege. All spent on betting, too. What a wicked world.

So look after yourself, Sir John. You are vulnerable. It might even be worth while thinking out an inner philosophy or faith on which you can rest when life demands of you, as it does of all men at times, steady courage.

13

WHAT WE HAVE, WE HOLD

THIS is a technical chapter, Sir John, but, as you are interested in keeping the golden harvest of your labours, as well as in the sowing and reaping side, I beg you to give it your undivided attention. You may know all the tricks hereinafter set forth, on the other hand there may be one or two that are new to you – and these may be very valuable.

It so happens that – by devious means – the Surtax Computation of Sir Gladwyn Hogge, or rather a copy of this rare document, has come into my possession. I will lay it before you. Frankly, I think Sir Gladwyn goes too far. As a farmer he is a phony. He does not know an oat from a barley. Sir Gladwyn, as all the world knows, and as you certainly know, Sir John, is plastics. There is not a plastic object in the market, these days, that does not seem to have the famous Hogge Plastics trade-mark – a rootling boar – stamped firmly on it. Your toothbrush, the handbag of your odd girl-friends, the plastic elephant that little Patrick adores, they all have it, the sign of the House of Hogge.

Let me tell you first how it all started, for the story

of Sir Gladwyn is, in part, the story of England, and the story of England is a strange story with witchery and cunning and beauty in its thread.

Way back in the fourteenth century there was a family of swineherd in Devon called Hogger. It was an occupational name. All the Hoggers were gross, fat men with very small, red eyes. They seemed to have taken on many of the qualities and characteristics of the herds they tended. The Hoggers were serfs. Suddenly, very early in the sixteenth century, it appears that an exceptionally able Hogger, George Hogger, was acquiring land near Exeter. The Hoggers had freed themselves from serfdom and, by an intense acquisitive effort, spread over three generations, had begun to accumulate wealth. How, exactly, this was done we do not know. but we do know, from the ancient records of the parish churches, that whenever there was a sale of land in the sixteenth century around those charming Devon villages east of Exeter – Payhembury, Clyst Honiton, Ottery St Mary, Honiton, itself – it was, more often than not, a Hogger who was the buyer.

The Hoggers, formerly serfs, became farmers, and then, in the seventeenth century, country gentlemen. So much so that when Charles II was unusually short of money he insisted on making the George Hogger of the day a Baronet, in return for a very nice round sum in gold napoleons.

A Cecil who was around the Court at the time – the

Cecils float like bearded ghosts throughout English history especially when there is an Elizabeth on the Throne – protested to the King that George Hogger was not 'a gentleman'.

'Damme, man,' said the King, 'what does that signify? He's stinking rich.'

So Sir George Hogger it was of Lynn in the County of Devon. Sir George got himself a very nice coat of arms from the College of Heralds, a rootling boar nosing his way through an autumnal wood with a fallow deer, couchant, in the top right-hand corner. Sir George also acquired the apposite family motto: What We Have, We Hold.

Now the Baronetcy became extinct in the reign of good King George I, and it was not until Gladywn Hogge needed to be supplied with the baronial accoutrements that the College of Heralds had, again, to look into the Hogge history. They were delighted to find that Gladwyn, through a female, was descended from that romantic and wealthy family the Hoggers. They suggested that Mr Hogge should apply to take over the Hogger heraldic lot as it stood. It had been in disuse for two hundred years, which seemed a pity.

So Gladwyn Hogge applied, and his application, in due course, was granted. His arms show the rootling boar and the fallow deer, couchant, and his motto, as appropriate to him as it ever was to old George Hogger, is: What We Have, We Hold.

Which brings us, from the fourteenth century, bang up to the surtax return of Sir Gladwyn Hogge, Baronet, for the year 1958–9.

This is it:

SIR GLADWYN HOGGE

Surtax return 1958–9

	£	£
Salary as Managing Director of Hogge Plastics (Import & Export) Ltd. ..		15000
Expenses reimbursed by Hogge Plastics Ltd.	19748	
Less: Expenditure agreed with Inspector as being wholly necessarily and exclusively incurred in the performance of duties as Managing Director (*See* Note I) ..	19748	
		NIL
Personal Benefits:		
Company's Bentley and chauffeur (*See* Note II)		348
Park Lane flat (*See* Note III) ..		NIL
Dividend at 12½% on 30,000 Hogge Plastics Ordinary Shares		7500
Wife's investment income		4940
Net annual value of *The Willows* ..	984	
Less: Maintenance claim as agreed (*See* Note V)	984	
		NIL
		27788

	£	£
Charges on Income:		
Bank overdraft interest	2064	
Farm loss (*See* Note VI)	5708	
Farm capital allowances (Note VII)	1872	
Annual payments under seven year Deeds of Covenant:		
Widowed mother	6460	
Wife's widowed mother	3898	
Grandchildren £1000 each: John, James, Betty, and Henry (age 2 months)	4000	
Personal allowances (Less £140) ..	300	
National Health contributions ..	26	
		24328
Total income for Surtax purposes ..		3460
Surtax payable January 1st 1960 ..		193

Now, Sir John, these returns may startle you, they are so bold and adroit. The cream in the coconut is that the good Sir Gladwyn, a very rich man, pays hardly any super-tax at all. But this is not accomplished without effort. The key to the effort is contained in the phrase, a significant one – 'as agreed with the Inspector'. There must be an understanding between the Inspector and Sir Gladwyn. The Inspector must assure himself that, legally, Sir Gladwyn's figures are above suspicion, and that, in any case, very rich, astute, City gentlemen do not pay full surtax, which would make life quite intolerable.

Sir Gladwyn's account only becomes easily explicable if you will follow these rather copious notes intended to elucidate the trickier points.

NOTES

I. The £19,748 expenses reimbursed is mainly for world cruises on the *Patricia* that include countries where Hogge Plastics operate, as well as lunches at the Savoy while in London, entertaining at home, and £100 a week for 'Sunday entertaining – weekend guests.'

II. The charge for the use of the Bentley is very nicely calculated as follows:

			£
Capital cost £8000 @ 9%			720
Two chauffeurs' wages	..	..	1040
Running expenses	..	..	986
			2746

Total annual mileage — 21,668
Total private mileage — 2,500

$$\text{Charge for personal use:} \quad \frac{2,500}{21,668} \times 2746 \quad = \quad £348$$

III. Sir Gladwyn's accountants agree that he spent 116 nights of the year in the Park Lane flat but that there was no benefit assessable from this because he only stayed in the flat when entertaining overseas customers of Hogge Plastics, and this did not reduce the expenses incurred at home.

IV. In fact as we know Sir Gladwyn and his family control Hogge Plastics. There are two million Ordinary Shares in the Company and £40 million A shares that are non-voting.

The Hogge family control 66 per cent of the Ordinary Shares. The majority of these shares are held by the Hogge Family Trust which, of course, is a separate, juristic, and taxable person. Current prices 89/6 for the Ordinary Shares. 85/6 for the A shares.

V. No Schedule A will be payable on the Hogge mansion for five years because £5,956 has already been agreed (!) as having been spent on 'sundry plumbing', in fact on the installation of an oil-fuel central-heating system.

VI. The farm sales are also the subject of careful calculation.

	£	£
Farm Wages (including butler and gardeners)		5364
Estate car running expenses	464	
Less: Private use	46	
	———	418

House expenses:	£	£
N.A.V.	984	
Rates	1040	
Heating and lighting	870	
Repairs and decorations		
(not including maintenance)..	2508	
	5402	
One-third charged to farm as 'offices'..		1800
Telephone		530
Postage		198
Farm materials		200
		8510
Farm sales	2752	
Estimate of own consumption	50	
		2802
LOSS FOR THE YEAR		£5708

VII Farm capital allowances:

Greenhouses, etc., for horticultural	£	£
section		846
Estate car:		
Initial allowance 20%	480	
Annual allowance 25%	600	
	1080	
Less: Proportion for private use ..	108	
		972
Sundry farm equipment		54
		1872

140

VIII. Sir Gladwyn's widowed mother owns a farm near Bosham and Sir Gladwyn often spends weekends with her in the summer, partly out of filial duty and partly because there are excellent mooring facilities for the *Patricia*.

The moral to be learnt from the surtax account of Gladwyn Hogge, Sir John, is that in a strictly competitive, free-enterprise world such as ours is, anything goes, if it's dished up in the right way. It's the poor what pay the taxes when they buy their revolting Crispies and canned peas and Ford Anglias. This leaves the rich free to lead us on to fresh export drives, new combinations, more enterprising exploitation.

You, Sir John, have a much better case than Gladwyn Hogge. You really are a farmer, well, a type of farmer. Your returns can be as bold, as forthright, as his. It is foolish to pay more than you have to.

So, Sir John, when you are cruising on the *Patricia* in Grecian waters, remember this little book that really told you how to work the surtax racket, and thank Gladwyn, too, whose account is a pattern of astute propriety. In the middle ages the owners of the land around Exeter, when Hogger had 'done' them and become the master of their land, found that they had no, legal, redress. The papers were all in order. We live in a world where the battles are waged by shuffling papers. See that you have yours in order, Sir John, apple-pie order.

'What We Have, We Hold.' Remember?

14

QUICKIE OBIT

YOUR story is now told, Sir John. You can, at fifty-five, begin to take things more easily. Your second son, Timothy, seems the type to take over at Gargantuan Steel. He's quick, cunning, secretive, but, as we elegantly say, 'Bang on.'

George, your eldest son, is in the Blues.[1] Well that suits him, and certainly he looks wonderful in that full-dress uniform he is wearing in the photograph that stands on the desk in your study. Your daughter has married a Baronet in Dorset. Quiet chap, never comes up to London, good farmer, loves Venn, his old red Georgian house.

I expect that, still, when there is something 'on' in the City, you will not be able to resist a profitable flutter. It can all be done by phone from the library at Canon Court. That is the fascination of the market. If you win you do not put down a penny. You go in when the account is opened and are out, before the end of the month, when it closes.

[1] Foxy name for a smart British cavalry regiment.

There are men making money now by following you, Sir John, just as you used to follow the giants, buying when they bought, and getting out just before they sold. A great game. . . .

And what have I to say of your record? What is the summing-up? Not too bad, Sir John. You have never lied or cheated. You have never caused unnecessary distress. You have, by your energy and brains, helped to give employment and a good life to thousands.

Above all, of course, you have helped yourself. Your motto – Entwistle helps Entwistle – is a frank acknowledgement of this.

And your personal life? How has that gone? You have almost forgotten, now, the casual mistress, the fleeting amour. You have always stood by your wife, and, yes, loved her.

If, after all this, she still loves you, and you have a few real friends, you may go in peace, Sir John Entwistle, Knight.